BOOTS THAT FIT

978-0-6482913-8-1

Cover design and illustrations: Meng Koach

RUTH AMOS

BOOTS THAT FIT

How to serve God and your community in a way that suits your unique gifts and personality.

CONTENTS

Foreword

Who am I?

My sister remembers that when we were growing up, all I wanted to do was get married and have children. I was sure that I was the kind of woman who would have at least half a dozen children whom I would homeschool with great joy and purpose. I was blessed to find Moz as a teenager, we were married when we were both 19 years old, and a year and a half later, our daughter was born. Jess was such a wonderful blessing, and at the same time, I found that motherhood left me completely disoriented. I did not enjoy being pregnant at all. I didn't even really enjoy being at home with my beautiful extroverted child. I couldn't understand it. I didn't fit my picture of myself. There was no way I was doing this six times!

After our son Caleb was born, I attended university in an attempt to combat the depression I was experiencing. I remembered feeling totally at home as I walked up the stairs to the chemistry building. 'I will be here *forever*,' I thought. 'I have found my true home.'

I completed my degree and continued studying until I had a PhD in chemistry. I found a sense of identity as a chemist, an academic, a lecturer and researcher. I lectured in chemistry, I researched, I supervised students. I enjoyed it all to a point, but once again, something was not right.

When I look back at my personal journals from those years I can see that I was feeling overwhelmed, overloaded and exhausted. Between work, church and family commitments I felt like I was going 24 hours a day, seven days a week. And somehow, simultaneously, I was feeling lazy and unproductive. Every morning I would start my quiet time with the words, 'Lord, help.' I didn't want to face the day. Something had to change. But I had a problem. If I left my university position, I would also lose my identity as a rushed, busy, hardworking lecturer. If I wasn't that, then who was I?

I really wanted to find my identity

I was told to 'find my identity in Christ' but that didn't really help. I knew that God loved me and that I loved God. I knew that I wanted to serve him for my whole life. But I didn't know *how*. I needed boots-on-the-ground advice on how to serve God in a way that suited my personality and contributed to the community. How did I do that?

I was pretty sure that God didn't want me to work myself into a nervous breakdown. I was pretty sure that he had made me with a purpose and that there was a way that I could please him in what I did without grinding myself into dust. I just needed to figure it out.

It's been a process. Some changes have been large, like getting medical help, and leaving my job. Some have been smaller, like using a calendar app and spending some time each day in silence. Gradually, my life has come more into focus, I have found my identity and purpose, and I have become much more peaceful.

I believe that God wants us to live in his peace – his shalom. Shalom, according to Google, means more than just peace. It means peace, harmony, wholeness, completeness, welfare and tranquillity. Doesn't that sound wonderful? An overarching all-round flourishing.

I feel that many of us could do with a few pointers about how we can find the thing God wants us to do with our lives. How we can build our identity on him and how we can serve others in a way that is uniquely ours. How we can figure out when and why and how to say 'No' to even just a few of the many, many requests that come our way each day. And how we can do that with peace and without feeling crushing guilt.

As we move through the seasons of life, each of us can have a time where we wonder, 'who am I?' It can happen when we leave school, or when we get married (or don't get married though we want to), or when our children become more independent and don't need us as much, or when we retire from a fulfilling career and now don't know what to do with each day.

I'm not pretending that I'll be able to solve all of your problems, but I have learned a few things in my own struggles to find boots that fit. In this book, I'd like to share with you what I've learned about finding a way to serve that is congruent with your personality and temperament, your values and your energy levels. About finding your identity and doing what is yours to do.

I'm no longer in the place where I start every day with an anguished cry for help (though some days I still do). Most days I look forward to what is ahead of me. It took a lot of learning, and some of the lessons I found particularly hard. I'm writing to you in the hope that it will bring you some peace and that we can all move into greater shalom and a more abundant life.

There are two sections in this book

Section 1 will help you find identity and a purpose for your life. A reason for living that fits you, that belongs to you, and that gives you motivation for each day. It will help you to clarify what to say yes to, and what to say no to; what is your responsibility and what isn't. It will help you to simplify your life.

Section 2 will then help you to live that simplified life in an coordinated and graceful manner. It is a 'how to' section, full of tips and strategies that can help you to organise your life and achieve what you're going for.

It could be tempting to head straight to Section 2 but I think Section 1 is even more important. You see, if you are going in the wrong direction, it doesn't matter how fast, efficient and streamlined your progress is, you're going to end up somewhere that you don't want to be.

Your life has meaning and purpose. I want to help you to find that purpose and then work at it 'with all your heart, as working for the Lord'.[1] In the process, we will simplify your to-do list, cut away activities, and bring more peace and joy to your life.

Ready?

"Effort and courage are not enough without purpose and direction". – John F Kennedy

---

[1]Colossians 3:23 (NIV)

Introduction

Are you doing too much?

How do you really know if you're doing too much? When you compare yourself with others you can feel like you're doing too little compared to some people, and too much compared to others. You can talk to one friend who will tell you that you deserve to take a whole month off immediately, and while another friend says nothing, you can feel the judgement streaming off them like a cloud: 'What is she whinging about? Her life is so easy.'

What are the signs that you may be doing too much? I found a really handy list of things to look out for:[2]

- Irritability or hypersensitivity (even if you're not expressing your irritation outwardly)

[2]from Ruth Haley Barton's *Strengthening the Soul of your Leadership*

- Restlessness – an inability to sit quietly or fall asleep
- Compulsive overworking – and this includes a restless quality to your work
- Emotional numbness – the inability to feel anything, either good or bad
- Escapist behaviours – Candy Crush, anyone?
- Disconnection from identity and calling – just going through the motions
- Not being able to attend to human needs – needs like exercise, eating well, sleep or even getting the car washed
- Hoarding energy – being overly self-protective in case people use up your last drops of strength
- Slippage in our spiritual practices – like prayer, self-examination, and caring for the body

Even if we put a tick next to just a few of the things on this list, we might be pushing against our limitations and doing too much with too little. If this is the case, we need to take stock and change things.

Idolising overwork

When I first read this list I realised that I had a problem. The problem was that I felt like these were signs that I was working *hard enough*, not that I was working too hard. It's a symptom of the age we live in that we idolise those who are workaholics, over-workers, busy people.

I enjoy watching *The West Wing*, an American political drama TV series. Lately, I have noticed the long, long hours that the characters work. They stay at the office until 3 a.m., go home for two hours sleep and then head in again for a 6 a.m. start. Or they just sleep in the office.

'Were you asleep?' a colleague asks. 'No, no. I was just reading up on some documents,' comes the reply. As if sleep is a luxury that *real* workers can't afford.

The characters don't have enough time for relationships. Their marriages suffer. They don't eat properly or exercise. And these are the good guys. The ones we are told we should aspire to be like.

This is not a picture of shalom. This is a picture of overwork. A picture of burnout in process. And *our* lives don't just last for two television seasons, or even five or six seasons. For most of us, our lives last for three score years and ten, and a few more if we're blessed. We are in this for the long haul. We are running a marathon.

We need to slow down and get a better picture of what a healthy, peaceful life involves for each of us individually. We are each unique. Each of us has different needs and energy levels. We need to stop idolising overwork and start figuring out healthy limits.

Imagine a life that is not filled with irritability. A life where we can really turn off from work at the end of the day and spend time rejuvenating. Where we're not blocking life or hiding from it or escaping into numbing behaviours. Where we have energy to give to others, and energy to give to ourselves. Where we spend enough time in our spiritual practices that we know why we are doing what we are doing, and even have the time to exercise and cook healthy meals.

It sounds like paradise. But that's the basics. That's what life was intended to be.

You have enough time

So why and how does life become too busy? Why do we end up attempting more than we can possibly achieve in a day?

I had a dream the other night (bear with me, this will be relevant). I dreamt that I was employed to tutor a student at the university. She met with me in a classroom and we started to work on her questions. Just then, students began to file into the classroom. The new students also had questions, and they were questions I could answer. I felt important and worthy; I ran from student to student, helping them with their questions. I was so busy going to and fro that I decided that the best way to deal with this was to stand at the whiteboard and teach the whole class. Look how helpful I was being! Look how many students I could reach!

Then, out of the corner of my eye, I saw my original student. She was quietly packing up her bag and walking away.

I realised that I had let the calls of the other students distract me from what I had been employed to do. That my one student, my priority, had been neglected because of all the other calls on my time. I left the classroom, caught up with the original student, sat with her in the hallway and helped her with her questions.

Our lives can be very much like this dream. We have a mission, a task, an assignment that is ours. But we can let other worthy causes drown out the still small voice of our own mission. We can get so busy that we don't even take the time to wonder if the things we are doing are ours to do.

Often it feels good to be busy. It feels like you are important and valuable. But it can also feel stressful and harrowing and exhausting.

Do you believe that God has given you enough time to do his will for you? Is God going to ask you to do more than you can accomplish? Is he going to give you work that takes longer than the time he has given you to do it in?

I don't believe he is. If God gives you work to do, even though it might look humanly impossible, he will also give you all the resources you need to accomplish it, including time. He is a God of peace, not disorder.[3]

What does this mean? It means that if you don't have time to do everything on your list, you are probably doing something that God hasn't asked you to do. What you are attempting to do may not be the will of God, or it may be the will of God but a job for someone else to do.[4]

When Jesus was on Earth, he worked at walking pace. When you read the gospels, you don't see Jesus running from activity to activity. He has pressures on him from every side, but he knows what it is he has been asked to do and he knows that he has the time to do it.

Jesus walks.[5]

Jesus also makes time to listen to the still small voice. When people pushed on him from every side, when crowds of people came to hear him and to be healed of their sicknesses, he often left them and went by himself to lonely places to pray.[6]

If you are feeling pushed upon by too many activities – if you feel like requests and necessities of life are pulling you in every direction, that you don't have enough time to do it all, and that like the White Queen you are running as fast as you can to stay in the same place[7] – I suggest strongly that you need to go by yourself to a lonely place and listen for the still small voice that will tell you the work that is yours to complete. This

---

[3]1 Corinthians 14:33 (NIV)

[4]This truth was imparted at a seminar given by Canon J John. It has stuck with me ever since.

[5]Canon J John again.

[6]Luke 5:16 (NIV)

[7]*Alice Through the Looking Glass* by Lewis Carroll

may be work that you do in your 9–5 job, but it may also be what you do for a hobby, or your ministry or service to the church, or something else.

I would love you to find thc thing that delights you, that fills you with purpose and energy. The thing that you can use (whether in a large or a small way) to bring life to others and to build the Kingdom of God. I hope that this book and the activities in it will help you with this process.

Just to be clear

What I am not saying

I am not saying that you should find your perfect job, say 'accountant', and build your identity around that. I am not saying that your job, your working life, should define your identity, purpose, life meaning, gifts and character.

Instead, let's turn that idea on its head. I encourage you to spend some time finding out who you are: your gifts and talents, the things that bring you life and energy, the activities that you find meaningful. Then when you know those things, use them to inform your daily activities. Yes, maybe you use them to figure out the workplace that suits you best, but also you can use them to decide what you will do today. Or even how you do the work that is on your plate today.

For example, you could do the work to figure out that you are the kind of person who enjoys creating order out of chaos. That's fantastic. You can apply that to all sorts of situations.

---

[8]Matthew 19:26 (NIV)

Maybe you decide that cleaning the toilets at church is a way you can use that gift to serve the Lord. Maybe you use that talent to serve others as a professional organiser, helping them to declutter their houses and bring peace. Maybe you use it in your position as an accountant, working with small businesses to sort out their finances.

Or perhaps you find out that you love entertaining small children. You might do the work to become qualified as an early childhood educator, sure. Or you might work in the church creche. Or you might take your small child to another friend's house and entertain her child as well while she gets some much-needed housework done. You might work as a children's entertainer, or take on all the McDonalds parties in your place of work. Or you might do all of these different things at different times in your life.

What if I have to stay in the job I have now?

Knowing your mission means that whatever the ups and downs of your life, you can always find a way to bring purpose and meaning to what you do. Even if you are stuck in a job that you hate, you will be able to think outside the box and find ways to serve God using your gifts in that place.

If you stack supermarket shelves, you might serve God by befriending everyone on your team and being a listening ear and support to them as you work. Or you might serve God by doing the work efficiently and neatly, making the finished shelves sheer perfection. Or by going the extra mile and helping customers who don't know where something is. Or some other way. God is a creative God and he'll show you creative ways to serve him.

What if I miss his calling?

I am also not saying that God has a job for you to do (say, being a high school teacher) and that if you somehow miss the signs and work in business instead, that God will have to scramble around and find a 'Plan B' and try to fix up your mess. No, what I am saying is if God has made you to teach, then no matter where you work, you are going to be happiest when you're teaching. So you may work as a high school teacher. Or if you go into business, you might give the training seminars to the rest of the team, or position yourself as a mentor. Or you might work after hours as a tutor in English to people who are new to the business.

Your purpose is not all tied up in the work you do to make a living, or in the volunteer work that you do, or even in your life as a parent or a carer. I'm not here to find a label and smack it on you and put you into a box. I'm here to help you figure out how God has made you and how you can serve him best. That might mean serving him in a new way right where you are now, or it may mean taking hold of the choices that are available in our culture right now and serving him in a new way in a new place.

What if I don't feel like I'm qualified to do what God is asking me to do?

That's a very good place to be in! You might have a dream or a desire to do a particular kind of work, but you feel like it's outside your area of expertise, or like you are going to be really stretched as you reach for your dream. You might feel like what you have in your heart is totally impossible. To that I say, 'With man this is impossible, but with God all things are possible.'[8]

As you depend on God, he can help you grow in your character, gifting, and strengths. You might need to do some training, or learn some new skills. He might even supernaturally gift you with new skills or abilities as you trust him. Ask God to show you the next step and see what comes of it.

Are you willing to put some time into finding out who you are and how you can best serve God? Are you ready to live life with more purpose and more joy, less irritation and less exhaustion? Then let's get to work!

PART ONE: WHO

CHAPTER ONE
Personality types

"Know thyself." – Delphic maxim

"There are two kinds of people in the world: those who divide the world into two kinds of people, and those who don't."
– Gretchen Rubin

Who are you?

How do you find out what your calling is? How do you figure out what it is that you're supposed to be doing with your life? This question has always been a big one for me. As I went through high school, got married, had children and so on, I struggled to figure out what the work was (volunteer or paid) that I should be doing.

If you turn up to any church, organisation or business and say 'here I am, a warm body, a volunteer, give me a job,' then you're going to get loaded up with work. But it will probably not be work that suits your uniqueness. It's not going to fulfil your deep need for meaning and purpose. You will be working like a sponge, squeezing yourself into various shapes to fit corresponding holes. You won't be working like a key, fitting into the lock that's been designed especially for you.

The question of where you fit best cannot be answered for you by somebody else. Not your parents, not your counsellor, not your pastor, not even your spouse, though all of them can probably give you helpful insights into who you are and what you might enjoy. And they can sometimes see potential in you that you may not see. But this is something that you need to figure out for yourself.

Back in the 80s, some schools had computer programs that were supposed to help with this very question. You put in some information about yourself, and it spat out the job you should be doing. I don't know what these kinds of programs are like now, but back when I was in high school, they were very limited. For some reason, whatever information my husband, Moz, put into the computer at his school, the program would tell him to be a fitter and turner, and that job is nothing like the teaching position that has now given him purpose and fulfilment. There was something very wrong there.

As I grew older, I turned to books to help me work out what I should be doing. There are quite a few books written on calling, and while the books I've read have all been excellent in their own ways, for me they have fallen short. You see, I've always wanted a book written especially for me that would give a succinct definition of who I am, and then say, 'the best calling/vocation/career for this kind of person is …' Of course, that would require some seven billion books to be written in order to satisfy the needs of every unique person on Earth.

Sorry to disappoint you.

I'm afraid that this book is also not going to describe exactly the person you are. Nor is it going to tell you exactly what you should be doing with your life. But I hope I can give you some tools that can help you figure out this big question for yourself. Yes, you're going to have to do some of the work. I can't do it all for you.

Congruent work

One idea that really helped me in my search for a career came from Eugene Petersen's memoir The Pastor. Petersen also spent some time searching for the right job, the right direction for his life. The phrase that stuck with me was that he was looking for a position that was congruent with his personality.

Congruent means 'in agreement or harmony'. I need to do work that is in harmony with my personality. You need work that's in harmony with yours. Work that agrees with who you are.

I've tried quite a few jobs that are not congruent with my personality. I've tried customer service, family day care, and lecturing at university. Each of these valuable and important positions exhausted me and brought me to the end of myself.

I've talked to people for whom these exact jobs have not been exhausting. I've interviewed people for my podcast *A Quiet Life*, who have found the jobs life-giving and joyful. Judy worked in customer service for thirty years at a local supermarket. She said that she met lots of lovely people through the checkouts, and that serving people that way enabled meaningful conversations. Kerry, who works with young children in family day-care, talked about the joy she felt that God was using her when she was doing something she absolutely and utterly loved. And Professor Matt said that, even though he is an introvert, working with others to solve important problems was the highlight of his university career.

When I struggled to keep up in those exact positions, it wasn't that the jobs themselves were bad or just too hard. The problem was that the jobs aren't congruent with the person that I am.

Eventually I realised that to serve or to work in a way that is in harmony with the way God made me is sensible, and not selfish or proud. That if each of us works in a way that is congruent with who we are, all of the jobs will get filled, and we'll all have more abundant lives.

And I'm not just talking about paid work here. Any volunteer work, or family support, or whatever we do with our time, can be congruent with who we are and life-giving. Or it can be draining and difficult. Yes, we live in a fallen world. Yes, aspects of every job will be demanding and complex, and yes, sometimes we are just in a hard season of life (more on this later). However, we need to (most of the time) choose commitments and activities that are right for us.

That means that we need to make an effort to find out who we are, how we are made and what makes us tick. We need to know what gives us life and what drains it. Once we've done that, we can move in the direction of the life-giving activities, looking out for opportunities to serve God and those around us in a way that uniquely suits us.

Personality types

Each of us is unique. However, individuals can also be sorted into groups where the group members share some likenesses. We can, of course, be grouped by race, height, fitness level and so on, but there are also many different methods of classification by personality type. These classifications can help us to understand ourselves, but here's a warning: These tools are great for giving direction, but they are awful if they are used to put people in restrictive boxes.

No person can be totally and completely described by a personality-typing tool. We are all infinitely more complex than a survey outcome summary can articulate. You and I could never be defined by one A4 sheet of writing, no matter how tightly it is typed. Nevertheless, reading the outcomes from these tests and thinking, 'that applies to me' can be very helpful as we try to work out which direction we should be moving.

The Myers-Briggs Type Indicator (MBTI)

I credit this tool with saving my marriage. Moz and I got married very young, and somehow at that point in my life I hadn't received the memo that not everyone is like me. I did not realise that, indeed, my husband Moz is not built the same way I am.

For example, let's look at how the two of us approach something simple like making dinner:

I like things planned in advance. Five years in advance would work well for my mind. I start thinking about dinner when I wake up, so that I know that I have all I need and can make the dinner easily when it comes to the evening. Sometimes I even sit down on a Sunday afternoon and make sure that all the week's meals are planned and settled. Then I can face the week with peace.

However, when it's Moz's turn to make dinner, he does things differently. He likes to go to the supermarket at some stage in the afternoon, whenever he feels like it, and get inspired by the food that is available there. Then he'll come home and make a masterpiece, and if we don't eat until 8 p.m., well, that's no big problem. The food will be worth waiting for.

In our first year of marriage, I was working full time and Moz wasn't. He would pick me up from work and on the way home I would ask, 'What's for dinner?'

He would respond, 'Depends what I pull out of the freezer.'

And my little anxious brain told me that he didn't love me. That he didn't think of me at all during the day. That he didn't even care enough to plan a meal in advance. I started to get very concerned about the longevity of our marriage.

Then we took the Myers-Briggs test and from the summaries we received I found out that while planning is part of my nature, Moz's personality is much more spontaneous. That nothing in the scenario I just mentioned had anything to do with his love and care for me. It was just the way he was made.

What a relief. And what a help. I calmed down a bit and our marriage survived that first year.

The desire to have things planned and organised helps me greatly now that I'm running my own business from home. It helps me plan and write books. It helped me finish my PhD in chemistry. It is a part of my personality that directs what I do.

Moz's spontaneity, on the other hand, helps him as he works with teenagers. He can step into a classroom and take each situation as he finds it, adapting his lesson plan as he goes. It's an excellent foundational characteristic for his vocation.

The other major thing I learned from the MBTI test is that I'm an introvert.

Now there are a few different ways to define introversion and extroversion, but the way I like to define it is that an extrovert gains energy from being with people, and an introvert gains energy from being alone.[9] I need lots of time alone to feel energetic. I am good with people, I am not shy, I can small talk with the best of them, I enjoy company and I love my friends, but I need to balance all of that with time alone. As much alone time as possible.

This means that jobs like customer service and childcare are not really congruent with my personality. I can do them, but I am left exhausted and drained by the constant contact with other people that is a requirement of these jobs.

---

[9]A good book for helping people to understand introversion is *Quiet* by Susan Cain.

Introversion is not something I can 'work my way out of'. My family lived in a community situation from the time I was two until I was 18 years old. We always shared our home with anywhere from one other person to 150 people (when we lived in a YWAM[10] community in an old monastery). If I just needed training to get energy from people I would have learned that 'skill' at an early age.

No, introversion is just who I am. If I want to do work that suits me, I need to take my introversion into account.

If you're an extrovert, you also need to take that into account. It's important that you fill your days with people and give yourself the energy you need to live your best life.

Introversion and extroversion, like structure and spontaneity, are points along a spectrum. We aren't just one thing or the other. I need people too, and sometimes I even like a little bit of spontaneous adventure. But knowing where we are, in broad strokes, on the spectrum can help us choose a life direction.

Enneagram

This personality test divides people into nine types, which it helpfully labels using numbers (making the whole thing a kind of secret code until you have done the tests yourself). To give a rough summary, Type 1 is the reformer; Type 2, the helper; Type 3 the achiever; Type 4, the individualist; Type 5, the investigator; Type 6, the loyalist; Type 7, the enthusiast; Type 8, the challenger; and Type 9, the peacemaker. Each of us has bits and pieces of all these things in our makeup, but Enneagram divides us into our major tendencies.

---

[10]Youth With A Mission

Enneagram tests come with a lot of helpful advice. I'm a Type 1 on the Enneagram scale. The advice tells me that my kind of people worry a lot, are attentive to detail, want to be accountable for their use of time, and feel the need to be perfect. They can take on too much, feel responsible for too much, and say 'yes' too much.

Knowing this makes sense of the fact that I overload myself over and over again. My personality just tends to do that. Now I can be aware of where I slip up and hopefully avoid the temptation. It also helps me to see that a detail-oriented job, or work that helps another to be their best self, will be good for me.

The Enneagram programs state that a healthy leaning for one person might be unhealthy for another. For example, if Type 8 (the challenger) changes in the direction of a Type 2 (the helper) it's seen as a growth in maturity, but if a Type 4 (the individualist) develops Type 2 characteristics it is seen more as a disintegration.

As with the MBTI test, there is great depth in this model. It can be viewed as a psychological tool or used for more spiritual discernment. You can take a simple online survey and receive some helpful insight, and if you want to you can find a specialist and work deeply into what this personality typing might say about you. I have only scratched the surface myself, and what I've seen I've found to be useful.

The Four Tendencies

This method, from Gretchen Rubin, divides people into four groups: Upholders, Obligers, Questioners and Rebels, according to how they respond to outer and inner expectations.

The Upholder has no problem meeting both outer and inner expectations. They do what others expect; however, they are also aware of what they want for themselves, so they have no problem saying 'no' to others' expectations if they clash with their own. They will put aside time to do their own projects, writing a book or running a marathon, even while keeping up with outside requirements.

The Obliger will meet outside obligations to the detriment of inner expectations. They will do anything they are asked by someone else, but find it quite difficult to prioritise tasks in a way to make their own dreams come true.

The Questioner questions everything. They'll do what you want if it makes sense to them, if they have good reason for it. But if there's not a good reason, they will not do it. It doesn't matter whether the idea comes from within, or whether it is a expectation from others. Questioners like to find better ways to do things and will want to improve anything they are involved in.

The Rebel only does what they want to do. As soon as anything feels like a rule or expectation, the answer is 'no'. Even if this decision is to their own detriment. They won't keep to a schedule, or work to a plan; they avoid both inner and outer expectations. Rebels get a boost from a challenge and show us that we're more free than we think we are.

In this personality division, I fall into the category of 'Obliger'. I find it very easy to do things for others, but difficult to meet my own inner expectations. For example, I have wanted to exercise regularly and well for years. It is an inner expectation that I have of myself. However, when I start on a new exercise regime, other things just seem to get in the way. I tell myself that these other things are more important and I push my own needs aside.

This was the case until late 2020 when my psychologist gave me an outer expectation. She told me that I needed, for my mental health, to exercise for 30 minutes a day, six days a week, with a heart rate at 120 beats per minute or above. It took a bit of time to get fit enough to do that, but after a few months I could keep up the pace. And because I have been instructed to do so by a medical professional, I have continued since then to exercise for thirty minutes, at my target heart rate, five to six times a week. I feel better for it, but I'm not at all sure I would have stuck to the plan if I hadn't been given that outer expectation.

I write books, obviously, and you'd think that the expectation for writing would come from the inner me. But in fact, I keep myself accountable to Moz. I report to him on my accomplishments. I need him to help me keep working. I'm grateful for someone to be accountable to so that I can meet the book-writing goals that are so important to me.

All four of the tendencies have their own issues that can get in the way of healthy and happy living. These are not bad or sinful things on their own, they just need to be worked with and adjusted for as we live our lives. If you are a rebel by nature, some work positions will be uncomfortable and difficult. But others will suit you perfectly. It's the same with the other three tendencies. A knowledge of who you are and how you attack life will help you move in the right direction.

But wait ... there's more

There are plenty of other tests. You can do surveys that will help you find your strongest spiritual gift (e.g., mercy, prophecy, service). You can do the Strengths Finder test by Tom Rath and work towards increasing your strengths rather than fixing your weaknesses. There's DISC (Dominance, Influence, Steadiness and Compliance). Or the test that tells you which animal type you are most like.

Each of these tests will have strengths and limitations. The biggest limitation will come if we use the test to judge and box others. The big strength of these tests is that they help us to understand ourselves better, and they can help us to have more empathy and understanding of the behaviour of others as well.

Sometimes we can look at the behaviour of others and judge them by the way we would respond in the same situation. For example, if I don't have a plan for dinner by 5 p.m. it is because 1) I am so frantically busy that I haven't had time to think, or 2) I just don't care about the people I'm feeding. However, if Moz doesn't have a plan for dinner by 5 p.m. it just means that he doesn't have a plan for dinner. There is no emotion attached to the situation at all. Knowing these personality types and really thinking about them, helps me to relax, as I realise that everyone in the world is not like me.

'Do unto others as you would have them do unto you', the Golden Rule, is a good rule to follow. But it doesn't mean that everyone is the same. Treating people with the same respect and kindness you would love to receive is the plan. Judging others because they don't behave the same way that you would in their situation is not the plan. We are made differently and respond to the world differently. Taking the time to understand that is a kindness.

Activities

Personality tests

If you would like to do one of the personality tests, there are many options online. Here are two that you can do for free if you are willing to give the website your email address:

Myers-Briggs Personality Test
https://www.16personalities.com/free-personality-test
Enneagram
https://www.truity.com/test/enneagram-personality-test

What do you enjoy?

One of the things I have found helpful when thinking about who I am, is just to analyse my own behaviour. Try answering these questions:

- What kinds of activities or work do you enjoy?
- How do you actually spend your time? (For example, you might think you enjoy a particular activity such as paddle boarding, but if you never get around to it, and instead you get out the bike and go for a ride every Saturday morning, then that shows you that you possibly find riding more enjoyable than paddle boarding.)
- What's an activity or task that you would do as a regular thing, even if you didn't get paid?

Are there themes in your answers to these questions? Are the activities inside or outside activities? Are they with people or would you do them alone? Do they involve organising and sorting things out or would you be making a larger mess when you do them? Are they more practical activities where you work with your hands or are they more cerebral and require you to think academically?

CHAPTER TWO
Values

"It's not hard to make decisions when you know what your values are."
– Roy E. Disney

"Values are like fingerprints. Nobody's are the same. But you leave 'em all over everything you do."
– Elvis Presley

What do you hold dear?

We've discussed the importance of filling your life with activities that are congruent with your personality, but you might run into problems if you are only taking personality into account when you're making decisions about what to do with your life. For example, you, an obliger, might become far too busy because you always oblige and never say no to anyone, and, as you are an introvert, you then become overtired because you're always doing stuff with people. (Hmmm... that might just be me that I'm talking about.)

There needs to be another way of choosing what you will and will not do. A way of choosing what to focus on or what decision to make.

That thing is values.

You want to live a life that is in line with your values.

Values define what is important to you. Your values guide your behaviours and decisions. They are attributes of the person you want to be. When you live according to your values you live with authenticity and personal integrity.

Defining my values

One sunny autumn week I took the time to figure out what I valued. Very generous friends offered me the use of their beach house for a three-day retreat. I was all alone, on an island, in a house with a beautiful view. I spent hours sitting in silence watching the sun set over the water. One special evening I looked to my right to see a spotted quoll. Magic!

The weather for that retreat was perfect. Blue cloudless skies and gentle cool breezes. I went for a jog along the beach each morning, and another walk, well, more a stroll or an amble, at lunch time – shoes off and toes in the crystal clear water. I read books, I listened to music, I wrote, and I worked on clarifying my values.[11]

The first thing I did (before I travelled to the island) was an internet search for 'lists of values'. I copied off two lists and ended up with about 150 different words or phrases that described things we can hold in high regard. Some of the words doubled up, but I didn't let that worry me.

I printed off the lists and cut them up so that a different word or phrase was on each piece of paper. That gave me a pile of slips of paper, each one describing a unique value.

Now it was time to go through that stack of values and divide it into three separate piles:

1) Definitely something I value
2) Maybe something I value
3) Not something I value at all

If I looked at the word and simply thought, 'Yep', then that word went onto Pile 1. That thing was part of me. I definitely valued that thing.

There were some statements I read and said, 'Really? People value this? Nope! Not me.' Those words went onto Pile 3.

The words in Pile 2 were trickier. I looked at those words and thought, 'Hmmm … maybe. I mean … in certain situations, I value this.' I didn't value them enough for Pile 1 but I valued them too much for Pile 3. They became the middle pile.

---

[11]This activity was presented to me by my psychologist. She'd told me that I should make decisions based on my values. 'How do I know what my values are?' I asked. This was her response.
You can get more of this kind of activity from https://www.actmindfully.com.au/

Once I had my three piles, it was time to overcome the first proper hurdle. The next part of this activity required me to throw away both Pile 2 and Pile 3. The 'nopes' and the 'maybes' were to go. And while I felt safe getting rid of the words in the third pile, for the purposes of this activity I had to let the second pile go too. I was only trying to find my very top values. So out those two piles went, into the bin.

After throwing out Pile 2 and Pile 3, there were still a significant number of values in Pile 1. There were maybe 50 little slips of paper there. I wanted to get that number down to around five values.

The sorting became harder.

I took Pile 1 and divided it again into two:

- Definitely me
- Not quite so much me

I kept repeating to myself, 'I really value …' and '… is important to me' so that I could remember what I was doing.

I reminded myself also that all the statements I was sorting through now were things that I valued. Getting rid of one idea didn't mean that I no longer valued that thing, it just meant that it wasn't part of the group of absolute top values.

I left the values sitting on the table the whole time I was on retreat. I organised them into a circle. I rearranged them into columns. I checked on them when I walked past to get a cuppa. I thought about them as I walked on the beach. I cut Pile 1 down to 25 values, then 15, then 10, and then I managed to define my five top values.

It was simple, but not easy.

I had three nights away. It took me two and a half days to cut my list down to five.

My top five values were:

- Peace
- Family
- Security
- Wellness
- Excellence

When I journaled about these five values, I found something interesting. There were two values in that list of five that could be incorporated into the other three. Which brings us to an important point: Words, like Humpty Dumpty says in Alice Through the Looking Glass, can mean whatever you want.

What the words on the scrap of paper mean to you might be very different from what they mean to another person.

As I wrote in my journal, I realised that wellness, to me, means peace in my body. So that comes under the value of peace. And I value excellence in my work because it enables me to keep my job. So that comes under security.

So I ended up, after three days, with three top values:

- Peace,
- Family, and
- Security

These are my top values, not yours. And these words may mean different things to me than they do to you.

I encourage you to do this activity for yourself and to work out your own top values. But remember, this list of values is supposed to illuminate things for you. Not to lock you into a box. They are to help you to live your life with clarity and purpose.

What if I choose bad values?

Whatever top value words you come up with, they are not morally good or bad in themselves. The goodness, or otherwise, depends on how you live them.

These values can be selfishly grasped, or they can be lived for yourself and others according to God's will. Your values are your great strengths and your great weaknesses.

For example, I could save up all my money, work harder and harder, and trust in my riches, my investments and my work to give me the security I long for. If I do that, the Bible calls me a fool. I could be as 'secure' as I could possibly be and the stock market might crash, or even worse, I could die (like the rich fool in Luke 12). What would my security gain me then? Nothing.

But if I place my security in God then I will be 'like a tree planted by streams of water which yields its fruit in season and whose leaf does not wither' (Psalm 1).

How do I work with my values?

Chatting about your values with a trusted friend, or writing about them in a journal, will affirm them and give you strength of purpose when you think about them. It will strengthen their position in your life. Writing affirmations about close personal values has been shown to improve education, health, and relationship outcomes, with benefits that sometimes persist for months and years.'[12] In difficult moments, you might find

---

[12]https://www.annualreviews.org/doi/abs/10.1146/annurev-psych-010213-115137

yourself thinking, 'How is this an opportunity to put this value into practice?'[13]

James Clear, author of Atomic Habits, writes what he calls an 'integrity report' each year to check on how he's lived his core values.[14]

For example, he starts with a core value such as growth, and then asks himself questions based on that value:

- Am I learning new things, exploring new places, and experimenting with new ideas?
- Am I questioning my limiting beliefs and trying to overcome them?
- Am I building habits that lead to continual improvement?

His answers then give him direction for the coming year.

You might want to set a date each year to re-examine your values, or you might just want to make a time for a cuppa and a chat about your values with a trusted friend. Living according to them is what's important.

It's not always easy to live your values

Clarifying your core values may bring definition to your life, but you also may find that it brings up some conflict. At one of my workshops, someone asked me, 'What if the business I work for holds principles that aren't in line with my top values?'

This is where the rubber meets the road. Where you will need to make a decision.

Your values don't have to be exactly the same as those in the business you work for. I'm unlikely to find a business with a mission statement that says, 'In this place, we value peace, security and the families of our staff.' But if you feel like your workplace values are antithetical to your own values, this may

---

[13]https://www.psychologicalscience.org/observer/the-heart-of-the-matter
[14] https://jamesclear.com/2016-integrity-report

explain some of the tiredness and stress that you are feeling. It will not ultimately be good for your mental health if the values of your workplace clash with the values that you hold dear. I think that's worth dealing with.

If one of your top values is security or success, the dissonance between you and your employer may be worth it. You might stay in that position to provide for your family or to support yourself. But maybe now that you know that the company's values don't line up with yours, you will have the impetus to take more concrete action.

I'm not saying that you should just throw in the towel, but you can either work to change the ethic at your workplace, or you can start looking for another job. Or maybe you can practise your values through volunteer work or through your hobbies.

And you can always pray. Pray for wisdom as to the right next step. And pray for change. You might be called to be the change maker in your workplace, you never know.

Activities

Use the values list to define your top three to five values. (If you would like a ready-made list, you can find one in the accompanying workbook or at ruthamos.com.au/worksheets/).

- Cut the list up so that each value statement is on a separate piece of paper.
- Divide the values into three piles: 1) I really value this; 2) I sort of value this; and 3) I don't value this at all.
- Get rid of piles 2 and 3 and continue to sort through Pile 1 until you have your three to five most important values.

Choosing one of those values, write about how you express this value in your everyday life.

If you're facing a difficult situation or a major decision, write a paragraph stating how these values could guide you or support you in it.

CHAPTER THREE

Your life now

"Life is what happens while you are busy making other plans."
– John Lennon

"What a wonderful life I've had! I only wish I'd realised it sooner."
– Sidonie Gabrielle Colette

What does your life look like?

When we're very busy we can just keep going and going, without really thinking about what we're doing. We're working hard, but perhaps we're working on the wrong things. We're making progress, but perhaps in the wrong direction. Things that are our priorities can be squashed into the background of our lives, receiving ten minutes every fortnight, and things that we don't really care so much about can somehow grow to take up hours of each week – just by accident.

As you read this chapter, I'd like you to make time to sit down and really think about what your life is like now. To think about where you are, so that you can then think about where you'd like to be. I encourage you to take a little time to think about how you are spending your days, how you are spending the time you have available to you. What are you filling your life with? Is that what you want? Does something need to change?

A mind map

One of the tools that I find particularly helpful for describing my life is a mind map. This tool can help you to see the activities that make up your life. It can also bring clarity – showing you something that doesn't belong in your life, or something that might be missing.

Now, I don't particularly like mind maps. I'm a list person. I love lists, I have lists on paper, lists on my computer and lists on my phone. I have a master list of work to do, a daily list, a list of projects, a list I use when I'm packing a suitcase … you get the idea. Lists are nice and straightforward. Easy to tick off. Mind maps are much more creative and scary – I feel like they can get out of control.

But when it comes to looking clearly at my life, a mind map works much better than a list. It helps me to see the big picture and to avoid getting caught in the messy details. Lists can come afterwards.

How to make a life mind map

You can make your mind map as simple or as complicated as you like. It can be pretty, with different colours and symbols, or it can be straightforward grey-lead pencil scratches on a page. You need to do whatever suits you and helps you to visualise your life. I'm going to describe a simple mind map, but you can feel free to embellish yours.

Start with a circle in the middle of the page. That circle represents you. This is a map of your life.

From that inner circle, draw out lines to other circles. Each of these new circles represents an area of your life – health, family, work, church, etc. When I first made a life mind map I had just begun working on novels and nonfiction and I hoped that this new activity would be important to me, so I drew a new circle to represent my writing. That was exciting and a milestone in itself, showing me that I could see writing as a large part of my life.

Draw out as many circles as you need to cover all the major aspects of your life.

Now, for each of the circles that you've just drawn out, brainstorm what is involved in that component. Write down each idea you have and draw a line from it to its appropriate circle. Then for each of those you can draw yet more lines and circles as needed until your life is defined clearly.

For example, for the 'family' section, I have written activities like:

- Keep in touch with family
- Budget
- Food planning and preparation
- Take care of the house
- Saturday adventures
- Make sure I have the emotional energy to support my family

There is no right and wrong here. You are brainstorming. Whatever ideas come to mind, just jot them down. You might want to take time to do this, you might refine it over a couple of days or over a week. It might be hard to believe, but you can forget some big important parts of your life the first (or fifteenth) time you do this, depending on how full your life is.

It can be tempting to leave some activities out of your map because they are 'too small'. I suggest that you put into the map everything that even briefly comes into your thoughts. You want a clear picture of your life as it is.

What the mind map might show you

If you map out as much as possible of what your life holds you may discover for the first time just how much there is going on in your life. You can look at the page and see at a glance why you're feeling so tired or stressed out, or why you can't find the time to do that activity that is so important to you.

As you look at your mind map, your snapshot of what life is like now, you might see some things that are not in line with

---

[15]More on this later.

your values. You might also see some things that you are doing just because you 'should'.[15] It might become clear that you are squeezing in activities that are draining to you because they don't match your personality type.

As you draw out your mind map, you might realise that you have nothing in your life that belongs to only you. That you have given a circle to exactly none of your own dreams or desires, because you are not giving them any attention. Maybe you are spending all your life on other people's needs. Maybe your life feels full of clutter and distraction. If this is the case, I suggest you put a circle for yourself in there. Add the special circle in faith that you will be able to simplify your life enough to make space for the special work that God has for you that only you can do.

How are you spending your time?

You now have a picture of the activities that make up your life, but do you really know how much time you spend on each of them?

We are very bad at judging how much time we spend on our activities. We are very bad at understanding time full stop. I think this is because our spirits are made for eternity.

We can't believe how much time has gone by since we last saw our friends. We can't believe how the weeks just slip away. Every year seems to pass faster than the last. Time spent lost in a good book just flies.

And at the same time, the days themselves can drag. Particularly if you are the stay-at-home parent of a preschooler. Oh my goodness, those hours spent with little kids can feel like years! Especially that last hour before bedtime. Or time spent doing an activity that you despise. That time can inch by. Minutes can feel like hours, and hours like days.

There are 168 hours in a week. Do you know how you spend them? If we want to find out, we can't just guess. We need to do a bit of work. We need to nail it down.

Track your time

It is good, every now and then, to keep a record of how we spend our time. There are apps you can use on your phone to keep track of things, or you can use pen and paper. In the activity book (and at ruthamos.com.au/timetracker) there is a simple time tracker sheet that will work well for our purposes. On that one sheet of paper there is a space allocated to every half hour of every day for one week.

You can get too detailed with this, but I think the most helpful thing to do is to mark down the major activity you do in each half hour of each day. You can start tracking right now. Start at the day and time where you are, and fill in each half hour slot as you go for a week.

Will you remember?

It is really important that you fill this tracker in as you go. Yes, it will be a bit fiddly to fill in the time while you're trying to make dinner or teach a class. But the thing is, when we look back over our time, whether it's the next day, or the next week, we fudge things. We think, 'surely we spent a bit more than 20 minutes on the homework' or 'surely we didn't watch TV for the whole of that evening'. We change our memories. In fact, our memories are highly unreliable and become worse as time passes, especially when we are trying to differentiate between similar events. Did you spend 20 minutes making dinner on Wednesday? Or was it Thursday? Was Wednesday the day that

[16]https://www.scientificamerican.com/article/our-memory-is-even-better-than-experts-thought/

dinner took longer to make? You have about a 56% chance of remembering accurately.[16]

This time tracker is not meant to measure what you think you are doing with your time. This needs to be a measure of what you are actually doing with your time. So as soon as possible after you finish an activity, write it into your time tracker.

When I'm doing this kind of activity and look at the final results, I catch myself thinking, 'Yes, well, this was not a normal week. I spent more time than usual on visiting with people (for example) this week, but on a normal week all that time would be spent writing.'

If you catch yourself thinking similar things, it might be a sign that you need to track your time for a little longer. Two weeks. Or three. Long enough that you can know for sure what a 'normal' week is.

We want an accurate representation of your life. A foundation that can allow you to make informed decisions.

This is another way to know yourself and it is just as important as the personality tests and values. Annie Dillard says, 'How we spend our days is, of course, how we spend our lives.'[17] Knowing exactly how you spend your time may open your eyes to the person that you are.

Comparison

Your mind map will show you what you think your life is. And your time tracker will show you what your actual days are made up of. The thing is, the two may not match.

You can colour code your time tracker to match the sections in your mind map. Are you spending time on one segment

---

[17] Annie Dillard, *The Writing Life*

above all the others? Do you feel like you need to spend more time on different segments? Is there a segment that is squeezed out and not getting any time at all?

Our time is our most valuable resource. We need to be careful about how we spend it. We need to invest it wisely. The gift of our time is the gift of our life. Squandering our time wastes our lives.

Of course I'm not saying that every second should be spent productively doing some task or other. Rest is important. Rejuvenation and creativity are vital elements of our lives, and even a little TV or social media time does not hurt us.

I really don't want you to feel guilty, not at all. I just want you to feel knowledgeable. I want you to know what you're doing with this precious resource so that you can make informed decisions as to how you spend your days and your one wild and precious life.[18]

---

[18]This line comes from Mary Oliver's *The Summer Day*, a poem about appreciating rest and God's creation.
http://www.phys.unm.edu/~tw/fas/yits/archive/oliver_thesummerday.html

Activities

Make a mind map of your life. Put yourself in the centre, and all the parts that make up your life around the outside. Make it as pretty or as plain as you like – this is your life!

Use the time tracker sheets (ruthamos.com.au/worksheets/) to keep a record of your days. Fill them out as close to the activity as is possible. Don't wait days and then think back. Fill out the half-hour sections as you go.

Colour code the sections of your mind map and transfer those colours to your time tracker. Are you spending the most time on things that you think should get the most attention? Are you losing time to distractions and clutter?

CHAPTER FOUR

Not just a brain

"I am not merely a soul and spirit; I am an embodied human being, and my body is the temple of the Holy Spirit."
– Ruth Haley Barton

"Being an adult is just feeling tired all the time and telling people you feel tired and then they reply saying that they are tired too."
– Aaron Gillies

Do you look after your body?

Before we go further, I want to change tack a bit and concentrate on something many of us would prefer to ignore: our physical bodies. It is tempting to brush right past this, but we are embodied beings and we ignore this fact at our peril.

The thing is, whatever we choose to do, we will use our bodies to do it. To make the best use of our lives, we need to look after ourselves, not just the spiritual, emotional and mental parts of our beings, but also our physical selves.

Brain containers

Eric Valor died from Amyotrophic Lateral Sclerosis (ALS) in 2019.[19] For much of his life his brain was still active and brilliant, while his body had almost completely ceased to work. He said, 'We are not our physical bodies, our physical bodies are merely life support and communication manifestation systems along with vessels for procreation of the species homo sapiens and whatever we may later evolve into.'

I think that many of us feel that way. We concentrate on our brains, on what we are thinking and feeling, and ignore our bodies altogether. We see our bodies simply as containers for the much more important brain.

However, as much as I respect Eric for using his brain to overcome the issues he was dealing with and for giving himself a life of meaning even though his body was eventually unable to move at all, I have to disagree with him. We, as people, are not just brain containers. We are more complex than that. We can't ignore the effect our bodies have on our brains, and our brains on our bodies. What the body does affects how the

---

[19]You can read more about Eric here: https://sites.google.com/site/friendsforeric/

brain works. And I believe what we do with our bodies also affects our spiritual lives.

Research has shown that the body and brain work together to perceive emotion.[20] Your body releases neurochemicals and hormones in a stressful scenario (whether the heightened emotion is due to a good thing or a bad thing) and your brain then interprets the body's response to decide whether you're happy or frightened. If a person has become physically paralysed due to a cut in their spinal cord, they feel less emotion about what's going on around them. The response of the body and the response of the brain are interlinked.

We can tie ourselves in knots trying to find the root emotional cause for how we are feeling, or the historical reason that we are the way we are. Sometimes the cause of our stress or tiredness or emotion isn't previous trauma or the high-tension workplace. Sometimes there is a purely physical cause.

Living with chronic disease

I experienced this when I found I was living with a thyroid disorder. I have a disease called Graves' Disease. Let me tell you, you know a disease is serious when it's named after the place you end up! Graves' Disease is probably not named after a cemetery, but still, you can't get a much more scary name than that.

The way this disease manifested in my life was that I felt tired all the time. Tired, hungry and anxious. I put these feelings down to all sorts of things. Work was just hard, that was all. Everyone was tense at my workplace and so was I. I was sure I wasn't praying enough, reading the Bible enough, exercising

---

[20]Amanda Ellison, *Splitting: The Inside Story on Headaches*, Green Tree.

enough, eating the right foods. There had to be something I was doing wrong that led to all this not coping, all this anxiety. I tried harder. I felt more tired, and more anxious.

Eventually I got sick of the never-ending exhaustion and decided to do something about it.

I found a doctor who would listen. And, you know, I don't really blame the doctors that it took so long to figure my issue out. Because it doesn't give them much to go on when you vaguely say, 'I just don't feel right, you know?' But this doctor was brilliant and she ordered some blood tests. And we found out that I had an overactive thyroid gland.

Your thyroid output affects everything in your whole body. An overactive thyroid makes everything run faster and hotter, so you eat more to compensate. (People usually lose weight with Graves' Disease, but I ate a LOT more to compensate and didn't.) Your digestive system works harder, your heart beats faster. You feel rushed, stressed and anxious as your brain interprets the fast breathing and fast heartbeat as a fight or flight response to a threat. And you feel fatigued. Just generally all-round bad.

An underactive thyroid also makes you feel horrible. Everything works slower and you feel depressed. You feel lethargic. You put on weight. You always feel cold. Once again, you feel generally all round bad.

Once I started treatment for my Graves' Disease, everything felt so much better. The treatment didn't solve my problem with saying yes too much to too many people. It didn't solve the fact that I was in a job that drained my emotional batteries. But it did give me a solid foundation to start from. I had more energy; I felt less anxious; I was able to cope again.

What I am saying here is, if you are feeling dreadful, step one may be to go to a doctor and get yourself checked out.

There may literally be a problem with your physical system that is affecting your mood, your thought processes … everything. And it's worth doing something about that.

The five pillars of health

My problems didn't all go away with thyroid treatment. Some of them were still due to the way I treated my physical body.

As 2020 drew to a close, I realised that I couldn't handle the anxieties that particular year had produced. I'm sure you remember 2020 – the pandemic year. And also, incidentally, the year that both my children got married. As well as other large life issues that I was trying to cope with. I couldn't do it alone. I needed help. I went to see a psychologist. And she gave me brilliant life-changing guidance.

One of the pieces of advice she gave me was a list of what she calls, 'the five pillars of health'.

These are:

- Exercise
- Nutrition
- Sleep
- Social Connection
- Time to Switch Off/Relax

I am not a mental health professional, and mental illness is a real and complex thing that often needs professional help. These five things aren't in order, but are good for your overall health, and will help strengthen you in whatever struggles you may face.

Exercise

My psych suggested (strongly) that I make sure I do 30 minutes of exercise at least six days a week. But not just any exercise. I needed to make sure my heart rate was up at around 120 beats per minute for those 30 minutes.

Now, I was not fit. It took me at least three months of trying before I could get anywhere near this standard. But I found that exercising for the sake of my mental health was more worthwhile than exercising for the sake of my physical health. Sure, I was tired at the end, but the buzzing in my stomach caused by excess adrenaline and other stress hormones was gone and I could face the world.

As I continued to do this kind of exercise on a regular basis, I started to feel physically fitter as well. It's a win win. And at the time of writing I can now jog for 4 km (slowly, but still, 4 km!) and love to go for a jog almost every day. I didn't think it was possible, but I've gone from being a couch potato to a jogger. And a happier, healthier person.

You don't need to jog. You can walk (briskly). You can dance. You can ride a bike. You can swim. You can cut the 30 minutes into two 15-minute blocks or three 10-minute blocks. Do what works for you. Something that you might find enjoyable once you're fit enough. But do *something*.

Nutrition

Eating well is important too. The fuel you put into your body is what allows the machinery inside to work well. Or, as we used to say in the 80s: garbage in, garbage out.

Moz and I go away for regular weekend adventures, and one memorable weekend I was in charge of buying food for our time away. I was very hungry when I went to the supermarket, and as a result, our diet that weekend consisted mainly of white carbohydrates. Chips, soft white bread, jam and honey, biscuits and cheese, and, of course, chocolate. By the end of Sunday, in fact, even by the end of Saturday, I felt unwell in body and soul. Lacking in energy. Just *meh*. And really craving vegetables.

We can get used to eating badly, but our bodies are made to work well when they consume fibre and protein and colourful fruits and vegetables. And when the stomach and gut feel happier, the brain does too. Our digestive system has its own nervous system within it, which is sometimes called the 'second brain'.

At first, scientists thought that what went on in your gut didn't affect your emotions or your thought capacity. They thought of the gut and the brain as separate compartments. But now they have realised that what happens in 'the second brain' can have major effects on 'the first brain'.[21] What you eat can affect your clarity of thought, your mood and your energy levels.

I discussed with a friend the effect that food can have on the brain. She told me that when she ate gluten her gut felt bad, and her brain interpreted the bad feeling as anxiety. This meant that she would sleep fitfully and feel uptight. But a gluten-free diet leaves her feeling peaceful. Her gut and her brain are connected.

Another friend told me that her teenage son came to her complaining that he was feeling incredibly anxious and he didn't know why. A little probing found that he'd recently drunk a coffee and a couple of cans of Mountain Dew. That would do it!

Coffee is a blessing straight from God, but it is also a mood-altering drug. Your body needs more than just coffee. You know what the best thing is to drink, and I almost

---

[21]https://www.scientificamerican.com/article/gut-second-brain/

forgot to add it into this section because it is so obvious. The answer is: water. Drink water. Drink it hot or drink it cold, but drink it. Water is the liquid that your body craves. The body is around 60% water and the water around your body is constantly being replaced as it is used to flush out toxins and salts. The body is clever at pulling the water out of coffee or sugary drinks, but many of us are regularly dehydrated and some of us even misinterpret the signals our bodies give us so that we think we want to eat, when what we really want is a nice long glass of water. Being properly hydrated is good for our brains, our skin, our digestion, our whole physical and mental selves.

The best advice I could give you is that you cut sugar from your diet; eat only organic fruits and vegetables; eat small quantities of complex carbs and good quality proteins and drink only water. It's great advice, but it's advice I don't take myself. You need to find your own way through, and for me, 85% chocolate and the odd ice cream or bag of chips are luxuries I really enjoy. So all I'm saying here is, don't ignore your diet. If you feed yourself good fuel, it will increase the energy you have available to undertake your mission in life.

Sleep

Oh how I love sleep. I do well on nine and a half hours of sleep a night. Moz only needs about seven hours. But however much you need, it is worth taking steps to make sure you get it as a regular thing.

When I gave a workshop recently, one of the attendees told me that it was easy to get everything done – all you had to do was sleep for only six hours a night. Then there would be plenty of time to do all that needed doing. I told him that if I tried that I would end up in hospital.

The fact is that most adults need between seven and nine hours of sleep a night.[22] And that most of us are surviving badly on a lot less than that.

There are many reasons for our lack of peaceful rest. The invention of the electric light bulb can take quite a bit of the blame. But you can take steps to improve your sleep. I have a list of ideas coming up in the chapter on Chapter Twelve.

Social connection

Social connection is vital, even for introverts like me. And not just connection through social media, though that has its place. Face-to-face connection leaves us feeling happier, gives us a deep sense of belonging, and gives a similar benefit to our health as quitting smoking.[23]

One of the things I have learned about social connection is that it is best when you are real with the people you are connecting with. If you are wearing an 'everything is fine, how may I help you?' mask then you are going to find all forms of social activity draining. Connection is the word here – connection from the real you to the real other.

I went through a time where I was meeting with people just to help them out. To listen to them and let them dump. I wasn't taking any chances with letting them see what I was going through. I was just there to help them. I had friends, good friends, that could have easily handled the real me and I just wasn't giving them a chance.

---

[22]https://www.nhlbi.nih.gov/health/sleep/how-much-sleep

[23]Julianne Holt-Lunstad, Timothy B Smith and J Bradley Layton, 'Social Relationships and Mortality Risk: A Meta-analytic Review' PLoS Medicine, 7(7), 2010, 14

When I realised what I was doing, I dropped the mask and allowed my friends to support me, as well as me supporting them. It was mutual, it was joyful, and it was far less exhausting.

If you find that meeting with friends is always tiring, I suggest you drop your mask too. You are allowed to receive support as well as give it. Friendships go two ways. Your friends will appreciate the chance to help you out, to listen to you, and to strengthen you. And then you'll find that you can help them, strengthen them and listen to them too.

Another thing I've learned is that not every social activity requires deep intimate conversation. As an introvert, I naturally veer that way. I find the other person sitting alone at the party and get deeply into serious topics or serious support. These conversations can be really great, but once again, sometimes this kind of thinking leads to me dreading social situations because I don't have the emotional energy for one more deep and meaningful conversation.

I think this kind of depth needs to be tempered with times of just throwing yourself into a board game, or watching a movie together, or playing sport. We don't have to go deep every single time. Sometimes just doing things next to each other is enough.

Down time

The final pillar of health is taking the time to switch off. Time to relax. Time to not have to wear the face or be the communicating person or workout the brain. What do you do to switch off? Do you spend any time in silence? Can you let go of the many jobs on the to-do list for just an hour or so in the evening?

I'm going to talk more about this later in the chapter on rest, but I believe that we need, as a regular thing, to set aside time to relax each day, each week, each quarter, and each year. This is important for physical, mental and spiritual health. If you've been running on empty for months, I strongly encourage you to make time for this now.

We are more than just our brains. More than just thinking beings in containers that can walk around and speak. We are whole people. What we eat, drink and do with our bodies affects our emotional and mental capacities.

Jesus showed us just how important God believes the body to be by becoming fully human. He went through all the discomfort and frustration of birth and growth. He experienced the 'terrible twos'. He experienced the frustration of hormonal blossoming in adolescence. He experienced cold and hunger and tiredness. He experienced the warmth of the sun and the satisfaction of a good meal. God knows what it is like to live in a human body.

Your body is a part of who you are and it deserves some love and attention. What it wants is good food, lots of water to drink, 30 minutes of moderate-intensity exercise most days, a chat with a good friend, and a good night's sleep. While this may seem totally unattainable right now, I hope that you can, even today, start to take steps towards helping your body be the best it can be.

And don't forget to check in with your friendly local doctor. I tell you, it's worth it.

Activities

In the book Getting Things Done, David Allen asks 'what is the next action?' Changing your physical activities can be a daunting task. Below, write three 'next actions' you can do to prioritise looking after your physical self.

1.

2.

3.

Make a date with a good friend to go for a walk together in nature. This will tick the physical exercise and social interaction boxes, give you sunlight (hence vitamin D), get you out in nature and hopefully contribute to better sleep.

CHAPTER FIVE
Limiting beliefs

"Comparison is the thief of joy."
– Theodore Roosevelt

"Then you will know the truth, and the truth will set you free."
– Jesus, in John 8:32 (NIV)

What does success look like?

I'm very proud of my father. What he has achieved in his life is pretty amazing.

When I was a child, Dad took a position as the administrator of a children's home. The home was on the verge of closing down. Things had gone very badly there for some reason. And Dad, who had no social work degree, in fact, no university degree at all, applied to run the place. They took him on and he turned the home around. When he left it was a thriving Christian community looking after foster children on site and off site, and looking after the foster parents as well.

Dad and Mum left the children's home to join a mission organisation, and after a couple of years training they were asked to come back to Tasmania and run the missions base down here. The base was small and struggling when Dad took it on, but once again he turned it around and it became a thriving centre for missions with two campuses and many staff.

The next struggling place that Dad turned around was the local Christian radio station. After that, he and Mum went overseas to help with a performing arts fellowship. When they came back to Tasmania, he was ordained an Anglican priest and helped to build the congregation of a small local church.

You get the picture. It seems that Dad's mission in life is to take small and crumbling organisations and build them into thriving operations that healthily serve God.

It's very uplifting, isn't it?

A couple of years ago, I worked out that when I thought of the term 'success' I pictured someone taking an organisation that's tiny, falling apart and chaotic, and bringing order out of it and growing it into something large and wonderful. That's what I believed success to be.

I wanted to be successful of course, so I tried to do that too. I tried to start a prayer group at the university. From start to finish, in the couple of years that I was leading, that prayer group consisted of me, and occasionally three or four others. Most weeks it was just me. Not exactly sizeable growth or a thriving success.

I tried to work with a Christian dance organisation. I could see great things for that organisation and put my ideas forward as I volunteered to be the state director. I didn't even get to try – they gave the position to someone else.

In fact, any time in my life when I have tried to mimic my dad's version of success, I have failed. Failed spectacularly. I haven't even been able to get the thing off the ground no matter what organisation or group it was.

Late in my forties I realised that the reason I could not make these projects into great successes was that Dad's version of success does not belong to me. It's like me trying to wear his suit. It's not mine; it doesn't fit.

When I realised that, I could look at my life and see that I have had success. I have raised two beautiful children. I won the university medal for my undergraduate degree. I won an award for my PhD thesis. I have published seven books (so far). I have started my own small business and made it financially stable.

But I couldn't see all those things when I was looking through the lens of Dad's success. There I was, wandering around thinking I was a failure, and it was because I was looking to make it in life, using someone else's success.

I needed to find the idea of success that suited me.

What's your picture of success? Are you viewing yourself as a failure because you are trying to live someone else's life? I've heard of people being squeezed into their parents' view of success, or maybe a view held by a respected teacher, but as you can see from my story, I found it just as easy to push myself to meet an ideal that was wrong for me. In order for us to find our own mission, we also need to understand what success really means for us.

Comparisonitis

It's not a bad thing to admire others. But it is a bad thing to look at others' lives and think that yours is worthless because it doesn't look the same as theirs. Joanna Penn calls this 'comparisonitis'. It's an illness that doesn't just apply to looking at someone else's success. You can catch comparisonitis in many different ways.

As we work to find our own rhythm of being, our own needs for work and rest, our own abilities and joys, our own God-given mission, we can start to look at others and feel inferior.

I mean, if I compare myself to some people then I definitely look lazy – people who work from 8 a.m. to 7 p.m. five days a week and then go climbing mountains on weekends. Or single mums who get up at dark-o-clock to go jogging before sending their kids off to school and then going to work themselves while simultaneously looking after elderly parents and volunteering at the local cat shelter.

However, I'm sure I could also compare myself to others who have different priorities or different health levels from me and think that I'm doing pretty well.

Comparison will either puff us up with pride, or hurt us with inferiority (which is really another form of pride). When we have real humility, we can look at ourselves as we truly are, not better, not worse, and this allows us to do the work we have been given to do.

Scripture tells us to 'run with perseverance the race marked out for us'.[24] Our race. Not anyone else's.

If you were running a long-distance race and you spent the whole time turning around to face backwards so you could see who was behind you and then turning back to check up on who was in front, that would definitely damage your performance. The same applies to our lives when we compare ourselves to others. Let's not do it.

Our harshest judge

Then there is the attack that comes from deep within us. Mine talks with several different voices and calls me all sorts of names. The names that hit me hardest are 'lazy', 'selfish' and a new one: 'boring'.

I figured out the boring one just recently. I realised that this was a core belief I had about myself that was really holding me back in my creative writing. I mean, no-one would want to read a book that was written by someone who is So. Boring.

Where did this particular voice come from? It took a bit of detective work, but I figured it out. I was in primary school when my father was the administrator of that children's home. My friends at that home were interesting, difficult, hurting children. They were (and are) all valuable people, made in the image of God. The one thing they were not was boring. But I was boring. I was good – a goody-two-shoes. Most of the time I did the right thing. The only time I didn't do the right thing was when I was trying to prove to my friends that I was not boring.

---

[24]Hebrews 12:1, NIV

In high school I felt the same way. One part of me wanted to do what God wanted, and firmly believed that this was the right way to live. But another part of me knew for sure that this made me boring.

Now, God is the most creative person within and outside the known universe. He is not boring. And following him does not lead to a boring life. Far from it! So these voices from my past, they are telling me lies. I need to stand against them and speak truth.

I am not boring. I am not selfish when I make decisions that maybe let others down but lead me into a fuller place where I can give to others from the best of me. I am not lazy, even if I need to nap in the afternoon, or to take a day off each week.

You may have similar voices that speak to you. Voices that maybe call you 'odd' or 'different' or (oh boy, remember this tone of voice?) 'special'. I'm sure you can come up with your own label.

Dealing with the lies

What do we do with these lies that have been spoken over us? What do we do with the lies that we speak over ourselves? How do we deal with these lies that stick in and dig deep, that hold us back from fulfilling our potential?

There are some things that we can do ourselves, and some things that we need help with. I am not a trained counsellor, and for some of us, that's exactly where we need to go. If these lies come from an abusive childhood, they can be built into the framework of who you are as a person. You're going to need some support to hold you up as you remove the lies, so that your life doesn't just crash in a mess around you. It's so worth doing the work, but it is hard work. You are going to need help and support to get through it.

If the lies are a little less foundational, there are things you can do to help yourself through them. The first port of call is prayer and reminding yourself of who you are in Christ. Spend some time in silence with God and listen to the truth that he speaks over you. Find those special verses in the Bible – Psalm 139 is a good place to start, and 2 Corinthians 5:17 – and there are plenty more.

Talking this through with a trusted friend can also help. It may be that you need a support group or an accountability group to look at this with you. Find people who you can be totally real with, who love you unconditionally, who can tell you the truth in love and care for you as you learn to see the truth about yourself. When I'm wondering if I'm being lazy, I know I can turn to Moz. He sees what I do each day. I keep myself accountable to him. And he can reflect back to me what I'm doing and let me know that I am not lazy. (Or let me know if I am letting the side down.) I trust him and that trust is really important for whomever you choose to help you with this.

Another tool to use is affirmations. Affirmations are small phrases that we repeat to ourselves to help us remember the truth. They can be truths that are accurate now, and they can also be aspirational truths. American Olympic silver-medallist Courtney Frerichs has used phrases (that she calls mantras) to help her in her career. Phrases such as 'Expect nothing. Achieve everything' or 'Be fearless in pursuit of what sets your soul on fire' or even a single word such as 'belong'.

Here's an example that you might find more relatable than that of an Olympic athlete: Moz teaches high school students, and at one stage, one of his students was having a particularly bad year. Things had not been going well for her. She had been struggling to keep up, and struggling to work out her friendships. But she'd kept going; she'd kept pushing through.

Moz thought she deserved some encouragement, so one day he took her aside and told her that the staff had noticed her struggle and really appreciated the way she was working so hard. She responded with a big thank you. Then she sighed and said, 'Growth is uncomfortable.' She had been repeating that affirmation to herself all year, and it was that affirmation that had kept her going.

Julia Cameron, author of The Artist's Way also uses affirmations. She says that when you hear that voice telling you the lie, find words to combat the lie, and repeat them to yourself, write them five times a day, write them out and stick them around the house and so on. Her affirmations include 'I am a channel for God's creativity, and my work comes to good' and 'There is a divine plan of goodness for me'.

If you're worried about which words to use, Scripture is always going to be there for you. 'No weapon formed against you will prevail, and you will refute every tongue that accuses you' (Isaiah 54:17, NIV), 'And God is able to bless you abundantly so that in all things, at all times, having all that you need, you will abound in every good work' (2 Corinthians 9:8, NIV).

There are so many good promises in the Word. They tell us God's heart towards us, even if they were not written specifically to us. I'm sure he loves it when we meditate on his Word.

As for me? I'd like to let you know that I am not boring. I drive a mini, I wear an asymmetric hairstyle, I write books, and I have an incredible sense of humour (for those who are willing to go with it). I am not going to let this belief limit me any longer. I am going to chase my own version of success, running my own race and not comparing myself to others. I am going to live life to the full, and I hope that you are too.

Activities

What are some limiting beliefs you hold about yourself?

What affirmations will you use to fight against them?

Write out each affirmation five times a day for the next week.

Need some to get you started? Try these from Scripture (all taken from the NIV):

- Take delight in the Lord and he will give you the desires of your heart. – Psalm 37:4
- Do not be afraid; you will not be put to shame. – Isaiah 54:4a
- Therefore my heart is glad and my tongue rejoices; my body also will rest secure. – Psalm 16:9
- He who began a good work in you will carry it on to completion. – Philippians 1:6
- For we live by faith, not by sight. – 2 Corinthians 5:7
- You will keep in perfect peace those whose minds are steadfast because they trust in you. – Isaiah 26:3
- Let us not become weary in doing good, for at the proper time we will reap a harvest if we do not give up. – Galatians 6:9
- For we are God's handiwork, created in Christ Jesus to do good works, which God prepared in advance for us to do. – Ephesians 2:10
- And my God will meet all your needs according to the riches of his glory in Christ Jesus. – Philippians 4:19
- For when I am weak, then I am strong. – 2 Corinthians 12:10b

CHAPTER SIX
Should

"There is nothing so useless as doing efficiently that which should not be done at all."
– Peter Drucker

"Next time you feel a should coming at you, ask yourself if it really belongs to you!"
– Kelly Corbet

What do you feel you should do?

So, you've looked at your life through the lens of your personality, and you've aligned your activities to your values. But if you're anything like me, there are a whole lot of activities that you're still going to try to do, because you've put them into another category. These are activities you feel like you need to do, even though they don't really suit your personality, and they don't necessarily align with your values.

These are the '*shoulds*'.

Shoulds are usually worthy and worthwhile activities. For me, they are activities that are highly thought of by my parents or even my grandparents. They are never things I want to do, but things that I'm feeling external pressure to do or some sort of obligation.

Here's an example:

Were you told, as a child, that you should always write a proper thank you note for every gift you received?

'But I don't even like the jumper that Great Aunt Gertrude knitted me! It's scratchy. I won't ever wear it.'

That didn't matter. Out came the writing paper and the envelope, and you were sat down to scribble out, 'Thank you Great Aunt Gertrude for the beautiful jumper. I will wear it a lot.'

And now, when you're given a gift, especially from an older friend or relative, you begrudgingly sit down and write a thank you on actual paper with an actual pen. Electronic communication won't meet the requirements here. Then you address it, find a stamp, and get it to the post office. All this, even though you've said thank you at the time the gift was given. It seems more trouble than it's worth and you feel resentment every time you think about the gift now (even if you did quite like it when it was first given). Now you decide that you don't even like it and are thinking already about where you could regift it.

You also need to take the time to buy writing paper, because you *should* always have some on hand, just in case it's needed. And you need to find a place to store it too. All to satisfy a *should*.

Don't get me wrong. Writing a thank you note is a lovely thing to do; a very worthy way to show your gratitude. If writing thank you notes and making beautiful cards and so on is your thing, then go for it! But if it's done begrudgingly, with resentment in your soul, and maybe even to satisfy a parent who has already passed away, then it's a *should*. You are really only writing the note because you should do it and for no other reason.

Where do *shoulds* come from?

A list of *shoulds* is full of worthy and worthwhile activities. They are all objectively good things to do.

They might come from your upbringing – a mother or other authority figure who told you exactly how life should be: Your house needs to be spotless and your walls must be painted every few years. You must make cookies from scratch; bought ones are not good enough. If you don't visit Great Aunt Gertrude once a month you are rude and selfish. You *should* attend church every single Sunday unless you are on your deathbed.

They might come from 'very good advice' you've read or heard somewhere: Your email inbox *should* be cleared to zero. You *should* spend time each Monday organising your week. You *should* write down five things you're grateful for each day.

They might come from your own imposter complex: If I don't read these five articles or apply for the promotion or do 10 hours overtime each week then I shouldn't even be here. Maybe I just shouldn't be here …

They might come from an overactive sense of responsibility for others. Little Johnny (who is 15) forgot to take his lunch today; I *should* drop it in to him. My coworker hasn't proofread this document properly; I *should* fix it up before management sees it.

It might come from comparison with others: Fred over there mows his lawn every weekend, that's obviously the way it should be done and I *should* do it too.

Rebellion

Rubin[25] says that Obligers will fulfil any expectation that is laid on them by anyone, they will do all the things they should do … right up until they won't. They continue to work and work, getting filled with resentment, until eventually they just rebel. They suddenly have a big 'no' moment and they won't do the thing anymore.

These acts of rebellion can be large and destructive, or they can be small and private. The person may get divorced, quit their job, or just eat a whole bag of chips in the parking lot. They just come to the end of their tether and stop doing the thing they know they should do. They may stop doing a whole lot of other good things too.

When I was younger, my act of rebellion when all the *shoulds* got too much, was to get sick.

I wouldn't fake being sick. No, I would actually become sick – temperature, sore throat, runny nose, swollen glands, I-need-to-stay-in-bed-for-a-couple-of-days-I'm-sick kind of

[25] *The Four Tendencies*, Gretchen Rubin

sick. It was the only way I could see to get around the list of things I *should* do, that I just could no longer do.

Let me tell you, this is not a good strategy. It is bad for your body for starters, and could have long-term consequences. And it stops you from doing the things you want to do as well as the things you only should do.

The thing is, we can't do all the worthy and worthwhile activities that are on our plates. There isn't enough time, and there definitely isn't enough energy to get through them all.

What's the solution?

That word *should* is a strong word. It packs a punch. It reaches right into the brain and overrides objections.

Here's my solution: Don't use that word.

In our house, *should* is a dirty word. When I use it, Moz will catch me at it and I try again.

Instead of using '*should*', I rephrase the sentence. I use a different word or phrase that indicates more of how I am feeling about the task and what its importance is.

Instead of 'I *should* phone that friend' I could say 'I'm feeling guilty that I haven't contacted that person in ages.'

Instead of 'I *should* do the dishes' I could say 'the dirty sink is really nagging at me; if I wash up, I'll feel more able to relax and concentrate on what I'm doing.'

Sometimes when I do this I find out that there is a good reason to do that activity. Then I can go ahead and do it with less resentment and more energy. Sometimes I find that the only reason I'm preparing to do something is that I fear my pride would be hurt if someone found out that I didn't do it. That activity will be thrown off the list entirely.

Each of us has our own list of tasks to do. If we add to that list the tasks our ancestors, our comparisons, our pride and our over-responsibility ask us to do then the list becomes impossible to complete. Let's throw out the *shoulds* and just do the tasks that are ours.

Activities

Write three activities that you are attempting this month because you think you *should*.

Now rephrase the sentence. What is the actual reason you are planning this activity? Is this now something that you can eliminate from your tasks or change so that you are not so resentful?

CHAPTER SEVEN
Seasons

"There is a time for everything, and a season for every activity under the heavens."
– Ecclesiastes 3:1 (NIV)

"Be aware of what season you are in and give yourself the grace to be there."
– Kristen Dalton Wolfe

What season are you in?

There are some people reading this book who have got this far and now, if they had the energy, they would take the time to buy an elephant, find my address, and fly to my address with the elephant just so they could drop it on me. They are angry.

And I understand, I really do. Because sometimes in life, all the mind maps, dreaming, personality type exploration, time management and everything else will not help. Sometimes you have all the right intentions, but the universe conspires against you and you're stuck in a situation where you can't follow your dreams and nothing you do will make a difference to that.

My mother is a concert pianist. As kids, we took it for granted. Didn't everyone go and watch their mother perform? Hadn't everyone's mother been recorded and her work played nationally on the radio? No, of course not, we knew that, but it takes a while for kids to appreciate how special their own mother's talent is, I think. I found out recently that at 15 years of age my mum won a concerto contest and played a movement of Beethoven's First Piano Concerto with the Tasmanian Symphony Orchestra. That's pretty impressive if you ask me, and there were many more triumphs to follow.

Mum's playing sometimes took a front seat, like when she and Dad moved to the USA for ten years to work with the Christian Performing Arts Fellowship,[26] and sometimes it took more of a back seat, like when we were young kids and she stayed home to raise us. It was always a joint decision between Mum and Dad as to which direction they took their lives.

---

[26]www.razoo.com/organization/Christian-Performing-Artists-Fellowship-2

But some years ago, the decisions were taken out of their hands. When Mum and Dad were in the USA, they noticed an increased stiffness and weakness in Mum's right arm and hand. Mum was eventually diagnosed with Parkinson's Disease.

This illness was really frustrating for her. She could still play beautifully and better than most people, but she couldn't play to the standard that she wanted to. The ability to give concerts and make recordings was taken away from her and it definitely wasn't her choice.

You need to grieve when you have something like that ripped away from you. It's not fair, and it's definitely not fun. But there is something you can do. I'll show you what Mum did.

She changed her focus. She still played piano, but she chose to use this moment to focus on another part of music that was very close to her heart – choral work. Mum sang in one choir, and conducted another two choirs.

Right now, this too is limited by her illness. But Mum continues to live life to the full, as much as she possibly can. She refuses to give up or give in, she gives as much as she can to others through playing and teaching piano, and also through sharing her wisdom and friendship with everyone she meets.

My friend Mandy is also going through a difficult season. She has chronic fatigue, and she doesn't know how long that will last. She can't do the teaching she'd love to do. She's stuck at home. Sometimes she can't get out of bed. Often her day's exercise consists of a walk down her driveway and back. But even though her life is very hard and frustrating, she does what she can, slowly and carefully, to celebrate creativity and to bring joy to others, sharing her take on life through social media. She shares photos of the flowers in her garden or of the shadows on the kitchen window sill. If she's got a little energy she makes a sketch or writes a poem and shares that on social media. It isn't what she wants to spend her time doing, and she'd love to know when this season will be at an end, but for now she just needs to live it.

Short-term struggles

Some difficult seasons last a shorter time than Mandy's or Mum's. In these short-term seasons, following your dream, working according to your personality type or living up to your potential might need to be put to the side for a little while.

I am an introvert who likes nothing better than sitting in a quiet room by myself and writing books. I wouldn't say that I understood this about myself when I was growing up. I knew that I loved sitting and reading and I also knew that I wanted to be a mother.

I married young and had children pretty much straight away, and when I was responsible for my small children, there wasn't a whole lot of time for sitting and reading. A quiet and peaceful writing life was not a possibility. Quiet did not exist in our house. I lived on the edge of exhaustion, peopled out, touched out and emotionally drained every single day.

I remember one night just a few years ago when I slept very badly for some unknown reason. I felt like rubbish the next day. I couldn't think, I could hardly move. Coffee didn't cut it. I was a zombie.

I said to Moz, 'I'm just not managing today. How did I cope when the kids were babies?'

His reply was instant, 'You didn't.'

And there it was, plain and simple. I had lived for six years or so as a total zombie. Living my dreams in that season of my life was not possible. Hanging on by my fingernails was barely possible. The days felt like years.

But that season passed and I learned a lot about myself from having children. One thing I learned was that failure is not the major disaster that I once thought it was. That even my little offerings might be of value just like my kids' pictures were for me. Having children taught me lessons that I have used to help myself on this writing journey. I'm grateful I went through that season, hard though it was.

My small-child season was only a few years. It felt like forever at the time, but looking back, it feels like it passed super quickly. I got through it, I learned some lessons, I received some joys. Then it was time to move on to the next season.

Moving from season to season

Sometimes it's hard to move from season to season in your life. It can be difficult to see that one season is at an end, whether it was a good or bad time, and that another is beginning. It can be difficult to let go of some responsibilities, even as you are picking up others. But it needs to be done.

My aunt lived a full and hectic life, working as a minister and archdeacon in the Anglican diocese here in Tasmania. She organised meetings, spoke at dinners, and threw herself into parish life. She loved the pace of life and gave her all to her ministry. And then the season changed – she retired. She said to me that she needed to totally give up on one season to move on to the next. She could have kept going with the services and meetings, with community activities and parish care. But she didn't. She gave the responsibility to the next person and moved on. She changed to a life of looking after grandchildren and enjoying travelling in a camper van with my uncle. She needed to make a conscious decision to change.

Lisa Terkeurst[27] says that we can't carry the weight of two seasons simultaneously. We need to release one to pick up the next one. We need to allow our children to leave home. We need to adjust to the energy levels we have. We need to pass on the work to someone else and let it go. We need to recognise and reorient. Holding on to the previous season, or spending all your life wishing that the current season would pass so that you can move on, these attitudes are life-draining. They are not going to change the season you are in, they are just going to make you feel less happy about it.

I'm not telling you to hide your feelings, push them deep down inside and tell everyone that things are great when they are patently rubbish, but I am saying that if you can look for things to be grateful about, or small dreams that you can work towards even in your current situation, it will make life more pleasant for you and for those around you. Bitterness is never a good look.

If you are changing seasons right now, or are stuck in a season that you really don't want to be in, take the time to grieve. Things are maybe not as they should be, or a beloved season may have come and gone. It is good to feel the emotions that you are feeling. Tears can be healing and appropriate. Then look for a little something to rejoice in, or a small way that you can show goodness or creativity in the place where you are. It may not be your number one dream, but it may bring joy to you and others even in the difficult season where you find yourself.

---

[27]In her excellent book *The Best Yes*

Are you stuck? Or are you just comfortable?

When Moz and I were in our mid-twenties, we had two children, a mortgage and a cat. What we didn't have was money, and we also didn't have much purpose. We didn't know where we were going or what we wanted to do with our lives and though I was at home with the children, and Moz was working flat out as a sparkie (electrician), we were both struggling with our mental health as we felt our lives slipping by.

It took a bit of doing, a lot of prayer, and a mini-miracle, but eventually we chose to go to university and study. I studied science, majored in chemistry and ended up with a PhD. Moz started in engineering, switched to a science-teaching double degree and now teaches in a high school.

While we were studying, we kept meeting up with people who would look at us, sigh, and then say, 'I wish I could do what you are doing'. It would make us sad. Because, for the most part, they could. They would have needed to sacrifice, they would have had to maybe downsize their house, or give up on overseas holidays, or stop paying for a cleaner and gardener, but they could have done it.

Maybe we made our journey look easy. We definitely enjoyed some aspects of it. Life as a uni student isn't too bad, especially if you do it part time like we did. One of us was always home to look after the children. We had nice long summer holidays (where Moz usually worked to make some extra money to get us through the year). We had flexibility.

But we also had very little money and all the frustrations that come with that. We had to budget very carefully. There was no question of buying lunches at the uni, we were taking packed lunches along with us. I had to be very careful how many friends I met for coffee. The price of a cuppa, even back then, was beyond our meagre budget. One time I rang my mother and cried about not being able to afford a tea cosy. It's not that I really wanted a tea cosy, I just wanted the opportunity to go out and buy something without having to justify it in the budget and go without something else.

So it wasn't easy. But it was worth it. Because we were no longer stuck. We were no longer watching life go by and wishing we were following our dreams. We were figuring out what our purpose was, and we were chasing it down.

Our friends could have done that too. They just needed to make hard choices, instead of sighing and saying, 'I wish I could ...'

Some people are stuck in a hard season and need to make the best of what they have, be content and adjust to the situation. Other people need a good kick up the backside so that they can see that they can, with a few sacrifices, change their situation and do the thing they are called to do.

The problem is that the people who are stuck probably think they could just change with a kick up the backside and that I'm telling them to try harder, and the people who I am telling to try harder probably think they are the ones who are stuck.

What do we do about this?

Please look at yourself with sober judgement.[28] Look at yourself as you would a good friend. What would you tell that friend? What would you lovingly want them to know? Would you tell them that they could maybe give up a few things in order to

---

[28]Romans 12:3 (NIV)

feel a sense of purpose and meaning in their lives? Would you tell them that an evening class once a week wouldn't be too hard, or that swapping TV for some other more constructive pursuit would be a great way to start? Or would you tell your friend (yourself) that life is already full of curveballs and that they should stop striving, be still, and trust God that in his time he will open the door to a new season where they can then chase their dream, and that in the meantime they can, in tiny tiny ways, still bring joy to those around them?

The last thing I want to do is to put more guilt and more burdens on those of you who are already overburdened. But if you need a little nudge to get out of a rut and into a life filled with purpose, then I really want to give you that nudge.

I can't tell you what message you need. Only you can figure that out. And it's hard to do that. I know it's hard. But it's worth it.

Activities

What season are you in? Is it long-term? Is it time for a short sprint? Is it an open-ended season? What do you need to adjust to help you get through the season? What can you rejoice in that belongs to this season? Is it time to make sacrifices and larger changes? Is there a small change you can make so that you're still following your mission, even with the challenges you are facing right now?

Write a letter to yourself, thinking of yourself with sober judgement. What advice would you give if you were talking to a loved friend in exactly your situation?

Dear Beloved Friend,

CHAPTER EIGHT

Doing what you love

"I originally thought they were all just better at pretending to like the things I hated. Later, I was confounded: why did they love meeting big groups of people and socialising for hours and throwing big birthday parties when I didn't? I thought that there was something deeply wrong with me."
– Jessica Pan

What do you want to do?

I was born in January. The middle of January. In Australia, that is the middle of the long summer school holidays. This made my birthday somewhat of an issue for me each year. I couldn't just take cupcakes to school, or organise an after-school or weekend party. My friends were unreachable, off on their summer adventures, at the shack (or beach house, if you're not Tasmanian) or on the mainland (that big island to the north of Tasmania) or even overseas.

Fortunately, we had a large family of cousins and for my primary school years we lived in a foster care facility, so there were children to spare, and I have many photographs showing children crowded around a table on which stands a cake from the Women's Weekly Cake Book, the icing melting in the summer heat, ready for me to blow out the candles. We played musical chairs and pass the parcel – in those days there was only one gift in the centre of the parcel, everyone else missed out. We wore shorts and t-shirts and ran around in the sun.

But I always felt like something was wrong. And I blamed the summer holidays. Obviously, I felt weird about my parties because I didn't have my school friends there. That was the problem.

As an adult, I felt confused when it came to January. What did I want for my birthday? I wanted to feel special. So I would throw myself a party. Lots of friends, food, fun times. And I would end up feeling exhausted and overwhelmed. Birthdays became a source of anxiety.

This continued until I realised that, as an introvert, a big party on my birthday probably wasn't ideal.

These days, to celebrate my birth, I might organise a tiny dinner with a couple of good friends, or just go out with Moz. And I really truly enjoy the way that Facebook helps my friends wish me a happy birthday over and over and over again throughout the day without me having to see any of them in person. Facebook has its issues, but it has made my birthday a very special and enjoyable event.

The media tells me that big parties with dancing and decorations and booze and rich food are essential. That I should strongly desire to attend big events, or great big music festivals, or even to watch a movie on the big screen with a large crowd. This is what I should want.

But these kinds of things are not what I actually want to do.

I'm introverted. Big crowds of people exhaust me. Small talk is not fun. Lots of sound and sight takes me a long time to process. Even a house filled with good friends having a good time is something that wears me out and leaves me feeling empty.

I sound like I'm whinging and I don't want to. It's just that when I realised that I don't actually like parties, I relaxed and figured out that I don't have to have one.

I don't even have to force myself to go to everyone else's parties. I don't have to force myself to attend every activity at church. If I don't want to do it, that's OK.

I guess, like Jessica Pan, author of Sorry I'm Late, I Didn't Want to Come, I thought that everyone hated these parties. That they held them because they were the socially correct thing to do. That we all went along, dreading the party, but wanting to show our love to the person throwing it. And then we all went home afterwards, exhausted.

Some people love big parties. Some people throw big parties because they enjoy them. (Yes, actually enjoy them.) And they finish up afterwards feeling full of energy and happiness. I mean, we can all have too much of a good thing, but for me too much is, like, one party. For others, too much is having a party every night.

There may be some activities you're forcing yourself to take part in, that you don't really have to do. If you don't want to go to the party, maybe ... just don't go. There are other ways of showing your love to someone, or giving your support to a cause.

You can send a gift to the person. You could make a time to have a coffee with them and enjoy one-on-one conversation. You could hop online and send a greeting, or maybe even buy a birthday card and post it. (Everyone likes getting something other than bills in the mail.) You could donate to the cause, or encourage others to donate, or make lovely crafts that you sell in support of the charity. You could pray for the charity. You are limited only by your imagination.

What if you could do what you love?

But what if you absolutely love parties? Or maybe you love creating special photo boards, or going on camping trips, or playing soccer, or baking. I know that I have found myself thinking that doing a particular task must be the wrong thing to do because I enjoyed it too much. It didn't feel like work, therefore it must not be a worthwhile activity, and I should drop it and look for something else that was harder to do.

However, a task or event or even a vocation that feels like total joy may actually be the thing that you were born to do. Can you imagine work that doesn't feel like drudgery?

There are so many jobs that other people do extremely well that I just suck at. For example, being a teacher is a job that I totally respect and value, and also a job that I know that I should not even attempt. Being with students all day, every day would drain my batteries completely and I would yell at the children, I know I would ... it doesn't bear thinking about. But I don't feel guilty that I can't be a teacher. I don't feel concerned that I'm not up to that position. I just mark it down as 'not within my scope' and move on.

Writing, on the other hand, is a beautiful job for my introverted personality type. It allows me, no, it requires of me, hours of time spent alone. It requires much reading and highlighting and taking notes. It then allows me to take all that knowledge and share it with others without me needing to see anyone face-to-face. All of this is pure, energising, life-giving joy.

For a long time I didn't look at writing as a possible job, because I enjoyed it too much. I thought that writing was everyone's dream job. We can't all be authors, I surmised, so that means that I can't be an author. Reaching for that career was like reaching for a shining golden star. It didn't feel like it was in the realm of possibility for little old me. Only the superstars were allowed to attempt to write for a living.

It took me a long time to realise that, for many people, a life full of reading and writing is like a life full of never-ending homework with no rest in sight.

When I realised that writing wasn't everyone else's dream, and that it was my dream, then I was able to look into whether writing was a possible job. And, you know, I found out that it is. There are so many options available for people who want to write for a living – not just novels and nonfiction books, but magazine articles, corporate papers, manuals for machinery – an endless array of possibilities.

Getting to know yourself and understanding your own personality type can help you look in the right direction for your work or vocation. Thinking about what you enjoy – that bright shining star – can help you to focus on what might be right for you.

Sometimes we don't allow ourselves to do something for the joy of it. We feel that everything we do must be of benefit to others somehow. That it is selfish to allow ourselves to do something that will have no short- or long-term benefit.

While it is important to use your skills to serve others, the problem with this thinking is that you can therefore never try anything new. If you are trying a new skill, you are not good at it yet by definition. If you are not good at it, you can't be of benefit to anyone else. Therefore, working on that skill can be considered selfish.

However, if you are willing to try something, just for the joy of it, whether it benefits others or not, then you will be able to practise it and eventually get good at it. And then, you can use that skill to benefit others.

When Moz invested in a computer in 1995 I was horrified. We didn't have money for one of those contraptions, and what good would it do? He wasn't using a computer for his job, he was using it to *gasp* play games! What a waste. No benefit to anyone.

But Moz enjoyed playing on the computer. He got good at the games, and good at linking computers together, and good at talking computer languages. And then, eventually, he became an IT teacher. He has taught computing to hundreds of students who have gone on to write programs and create apps and work with information systems and help hundreds of other people. And all of this helping came from his experimentation with computers back at the dawn of the internet. I'm glad he didn't listen to me.

You might not be able to figure out right now how this thing you enjoy will be able to benefit others. You might just enjoy doing it. I think that's fine. I mean, sure, fulfil your obligations to others too – make sure your children are fed and clothed, and attend your work during work hours. But also, make time to play, to experience joy, to experience fun. You and God can figure out together how this new skill will benefit others later.

Dream

You probably have a dream tucked away somewhere inside of you, and I believe that you will bless both yourself and others if you make time to let that dream breathe.

It might be writing, baking, playing sport, drawing. You might have a dream to run your own business. You might have a dream to study.

You might think, 'I can't do that. There isn't time. And I can't afford it.'

But I think you can.

It's all about choices. And maybe it's about thinking outside the box.

If you can't afford to go to university, you can afford to go to your local library and start to research that thing you are interested in. You can find online courses for just about anything. Because the goal is to learn, not just to get the piece of paper, right?

If you can't afford to quit your job and become a writer (and who can?) you can write in the edges of your day. Put aside 15 minutes here and there to get some writing done.

You may have to wake up slightly earlier, or go to bed slightly later. Or you may have to delete a social media app or two off your phone and use the time for something else instead.

We will talk strategy later, but for now, I encourage you to make the time to dream. It's impossible to put time aside to work towards your dream if you don't even know what it is.

A dream is a big shiny city on a hill. It is something to work towards over the course of your whole life, not just over the next couple of years. It's something that feels totally impossible. Something you will need God to come through for. It's something that's there, lurking in the back of your mind, but you won't let yourself think of it because it's just too crazy.

That dream. Let it out. Ponder it.

My niece dreams of competing in the equestrian events in the Olympic games.

I dream of making a living from my writing.

A friend of mine dreams of working with budding worship leaders at church and helping them improve in song leading and song writing.

One word of warning

Make sure this dream is your own. Don't go chasing down a dream that will prove to your father that you can be the success he didn't believe you could be. Don't try to prove something to your grade three teacher who always thought you were a failure. This is not about you 'showing them', this is about you becoming you.

A life spent chasing down a dream that doesn't really belong to you is a life spent in resentment and drivenness. This is not the restful, quiet life we are aiming for here. Remember to reach for your own success.

It might take quite a while to figure out what your dream is. Activities like working out your personality type, your values, and making that mind map of your life as it is now, and maybe one of your life as you'd like it to be, can help.

Another activity that could help is to write for yourself a story of your perfect day. What would it look like? Would you wake up early and spend the day climbing a cliff face? Would it be spent in the company of family playing board games? Would you prefer to spend your perfect day sipping coffee and writing in a café by the beach? Or would you rather spend it in the busy bustle of an operating theatre, saving the life of a patient? Be creative, be outlandish. This is your perfect day.

Try writing a perfect work day and a perfect holiday. How do they differ? What are the common threads?

What depends on you and what depends on others in this perfect day?

I know that we are fed through advertising the idea that the perfect day for everyone is a day spent in a tropical paradise, sitting by a pool, sipping a cocktail. But is that really the end objective of life?

When I was younger, my family spent six weeks in Vanuatu on a missions trip. I fell in love with the place. And I especially fell in love with a resort called the Iririki Island Resort. This beautiful resort is built on a small island in the harbour of Port Vila. It is only accessible by ferry. We didn't stay there; however, my mother would go over to the island and give piano concerts for the guests and we would keep her company.

As I sat in the audience listening to my mother play, I looked at the luxury of the hotel, the restaurant, the swimming pools, and the little cabins with balconies that jutted out over the water so that you could stand on them and feed the tropical fish.

I thought, 'This is where I'm coming for my honeymoon.'

But Moz and I got married at 19 years of age. We were so young, and we were so very poor. Our honeymoon was spent at my uncle's beach house and I am very grateful to him for the loan of that special place, but it wasn't the honeymoon I had planned.

So we did the next best thing. On our 20th wedding anniversary, we booked a holiday at the Iririki Island Resort. Now was the time to have that perfect, lie-by-the-pool experience.

But as we planned for our second honeymoon we both realised that two weeks spent at that resort would not be the height of joy and fun for us. We realised that after a few days we would get bored. We still didn't have enough money for adventure activities like diving and helicopter flights, and even if we did, those activities would not be enough. We needed more.

So we planned a few days at the resort, then we made enquiries about volunteering opportunities on the island, found a YWAM base that would have us, and spent time teaching in schools, building water tanks, babysitting, and generally helping out. We made life-long friends and we totally enjoyed ourselves. Except for the spiders, bugs, snakes and centipedes. But that's another story.

This is why I suggest you write about a perfect holiday, and a perfect work day. Holidays are essential (more on this later) but we are made to work, we are built for community and designed to serve others. Sitting by the beach is great for rest and renewal, but if we just sit, we lack meaning in our lives. And meaning is essential for us.

Kelly McGonigal, a stress researcher, said in a 2013 TED talk, 'chasing meaning is better for your health than trying to avoid discomfort … go after what creates meaning in your life and then trust yourself to handle the stress that follows.'

Doing what you don't want to do

I would really like to tell you to cut out of your life everything you don't enjoy, and to only do the things you really truly love.

However, there is a little bit more to living a full life than that.

Every job has some mundanity in it, some hard things that just aren't filled with lightness and joy. Yes, this applies even to your wonderful dream job. The earth is filled with thistles and the digging of it can sometimes be hard, even if overall the garden gives you great joy.[29]

Sometimes you choose to do things that you don't love. Things that are not taking you closer to your goals or benefiting you at all. Sometimes that is the right thing to do.

I had a friend whose name was Jill. I have written about her in a previous book.[30] She was a very hard woman to love. She was someone whose company I did not enjoy. However, I would, periodically, grasp at my courage and take the time to go and visit her.

Visiting Jill didn't move me further towards my dreams. It took time away from my writing.

Visiting Jill didn't fill up my energy tank. It totally exhausted me and often made me angry and frustrated.

Visiting Jill was not something I enjoyed at all. Not like reading a book or even the hard slog of going for a run.

The visits often felt pointless and annoying.

But Jill had been placed in my life for me to learn to love. I felt that this hard thing that I did not enjoy was a thing I needed to do. I learned a lot from visiting Jill, and all the things I have said previously say more about my attitude and my need to change than they say about my friend Jill.

---

[29]Genesis 3:17–19

[30]*My Year of Saying No*

Sometimes there are hard things that I need to do. Things that fit my values, even though they don't match beautifully with my personality, dream, or even the season I might be in. These things need to be thought through and prayed about. I need to make sure I'm doing them for the right reasons. And then, often, I just need to do them. Whether I have a good attitude about them or not.

Life isn't ever going to be one long sojourn on Cloud 9. We live in a fallen world. Some people rub us up the wrong way. Some tasks just need doing. We can adjust some things in our lives so that they work better with what we want to achieve, but we can't remove every irritant and maybe we shouldn't even try to. Some of those irritants are there specifically to help us grow. Some are just there. Not for a good reason, just because they are.

Figuring out what to cut from your life and what to leave in is not necessarily an easy task. Some things are obvious but others are not. You need to work and pray through each decision as you find your way along the path.

Contentment vs. Satisfaction

With all this talk about chasing after dreams and looking at the idea of your perfect life, you might ask, 'But aren't we supposed to be content? Isn't that what we're aiming for? Isn't it bad to be constantly chasing something in the future? Aren't we supposed to be living in the now?'

And my answer is, 'Yes … and no.'

When I worked at the university I got very frustrated that I was continually being asked to reach for something more. I needed to apply for promotions, apply for awards, improve, exceed expectations, keep pushing. I thought, 'Can't I just do the job I have and do it well?'

Then I realised that my activity depended on me. If I didn't want to apply for a promotion, I could just not apply. There was not much anyone could do about it if I didn't fill in the paperwork. I settled down to doing my own job as well as I could do it, and let the rest go hang.

I remember very well the day I realised that my plan to 'just do my job', to just be content with where I was, wasn't working. I was sitting in a seminar, letting my mind wander, and I realised that I was bored. With no forward momentum I felt like I was going nowhere. I needed a goal to reach for.

I was listening to a running podcast the other day. This particular episode was about making progress. The host was making the point that success isn't linear, and that perhaps we don't need to make progress in every activity all the time. The host asked, 'Do you always want to make progress in making your bed? Do you need to make it better every time? How about cleaning your teeth? Drinking a glass of water?' My answer to these questions was, 'yes'. I think I could get better at those things (yes, even at not spilling my water when I drink it too fast) and occasionally I make a conscious effort to improve them. Maybe I have an issue here, but I really like to make progress and to aim for a goal. I am a goal-oriented person.

It's important, however, to make sure that when we're measuring progress, we're measuring something that we have control over. For example, it is better to measure how many days you have exercised each week than to measure whether you have lost weight today. One thing is (mostly) under your control, the other is subject to so many different hormonal and weather and food and drink factors that using it as a yardstick becomes very frustrating. We will talk more about this later.

There is a difference between feeling contentment and feeling satisfied. One can be felt even while you are moving forward. The other requires a full stop.

I believe that we need to keep our contentment and our forward momentum in a kind of tension. We need to know we are going somewhere, but we need to move towards that goal with a heart of gratitude and contentment for what we have along the way.

Activities

Write a paragraph or draw a picture that describes your perfect holiday. What would you do just for fun?

Write a paragraph or draw a picture that describes your perfect work day.

CHAPTER NINE
Rhythms

"*Walk with me and work with me — watch how I do it. Learn the unforced rhythms of grace.*"
– Jesus (Matthew 11:29 (MSG))

"*Happiness is not a matter of intensity but of balance, order, rhythm and harmony.*"
– Thomas Merton

Have you built rhythms in?

As I write this, it's the end of November and I can feel the pace of life picking up as we move into the Christmas rush. I've had a few peaceful weeks where I've been able to write to my heart's content, get the housework done, and still have time to read. But all that is changing. There are more activities to attend, there is more shopping and preparation to do, and my editing work has picked up too. Every day is holding more.

I could panic. But I don't need to. I know that this too will pass and I have holidays already booked in January.

As well as the longer-term seasons I talked about in the last chapter, life has shorter term weather events. Storms of busyness and long summer days of peace. There are smaller ups and downs as well as the big life changes we can go through. And it would be ridiculous to suggest that we could spend every day in a state of blissed out peace as we lie on our hammock and holiday all the time.

In fact, if we're not willing to push ourselves on occasion, we're going to miss out on so much that life holds for us. Living life always on the edge, where we're always doing too much, never taking the time to sleep and rest and always busy, busy, busy, that kind of life is not good for us. But at the same time, always living slowly, never pushing ourselves, and never attempting anything just in case it's too big is not good for us either.

What we're aiming for over the course of a year is that most days are pleasantly full with a nice number of tasks, a good amount of space in between appointments, and our priorities neatly taken care of. Then we want some days that are quieter, filled with lazy joy – holidays. These days are spent sitting and reading in front of the fire in winter, or out walking along the beach in summer. Or biking or doing crafts, or solving jigsaw puzzles; whatever doesn't feel like work to you. And finally, some times in the year are busier. In these 'push times' we will have days that are full, maybe even overfull. These are days when we're preparing for a special occasion, or when work gets super heavy as a project nears a deadline.

This kind of short-term busy-ness is not bad for us. It's good to feel stress occasionally. It's amazing when you push yourself hard, right to the edge, and you achieve what you were aiming for and get that big surge of satisfaction.

An imposed rhythm

I loved my university days. Moz and I went to university a little later than is usual. We had been married for several years by then and had two beautiful children, so we had to cope with slightly different issues from those of the normal university student. But I still loved that season. I loved the ebb and flow of the university year. After a nice long summer holiday when my brain could totally clock out and rest I would enter the semester excited for what was ahead, new notebooks purchased, pencils sharpened. I threw myself into the study and Moz did too.

We took it in turns to come home early and pick the kids up from school. We slowly let things around the house go as the semester ramped up and assignments became due. By the end of the 14 weeks of semester all four of us were exhausted. The dinner table filled up with text books and notes as Moz and I studied more and more. We ate simple meals. (Did you know that kids are totally happy to eat cheese on toast for dinner?) We pushed through, studying at nights and on weekends. (In church one Sunday I wrote out the biosynthesis of morphine on the back of a church newsletter when I should have been listening to the sermon.)

Then came exams. All the information that had been squashed into my brain was vomited up again onto the exam paper. The relief grew as subject by subject I closed the books and packed them away.

And then came the wonder of holidays.

We would pull the kids out of school for a couple of days and head off to Moz's family beach house. We'd get to know our children again, apologising for what they'd had to put up with through the exam period. We'd totally relax, enjoy the space, and reconnect with each other.

After a few short weeks of break time it would all start again.

That particular life rhythm was artificially induced, but this is pretty much how I think it should work. Life should hold some busy times, and some quiet times.[31]

Busy-creep

It feels like all too often we experience 'busy-creep'. The boss asks for a special push for a special reason and everyone works long days at high speed and pulls off the impossible. Then the boss realises what can be achieved with everyone working at that pace and they call for it again and again, and then the high-speed, high-tension pace becomes the normal way of life.

It's not just the boss. You can do this to yourself too. It's all too easy to think, 'Well, I managed to fit all that in last

---

[31]I think God feels the same. In his calendar for the people of Israel, he didn't just implement the sabbath – the day of rest each week, he also placed a whole lot of different festivals in the calendar: the New Moons, the Festival of Unleavened Bread, the Festival of Weeks and the Festival of Tabernacles (2 Chronicles 8:13). All these festivals were times to stop working, to rest, and to worship the Lord. He put all these in place to regulate the rhythms of his people.

week, I'll do it again this week.' I find, though, that busy-creep happens more when I don't pay attention. I forget to put aside time to rest. I forget that it takes time to travel from one place to another. I squeeze in a meeting here, or an extra task there. I take on projects purely because they are urgent or I put some shoulds back onto my to-do list. Suddenly I'm running hither and thither, frantic and stressed, and for no good reason.

When huge 'push yourself' days become the norm, that's problematic. You can feel like you're pushing yourself for months on end and that the quieter days never come around.

Let me say again, short-term busy-ness is fine. But how do you stop this busy-ness becoming a way of life?

I am not perfect at this, but I think that the solution is to proactively book rhythm into your life. This includes daily rhythms of rest and activity, weekly rhythms, and longer holidays as well. We need to make sure that we prioritise rest.

Part of the problem with busy-creep is that when it happens, you don't have time to notice that it is happening. It just creeps up. Then one day you realise how frazzled you are, and you look at your calendar and find that you are booked to continue to be frazzled for the foreseeable future.

By booking in holidays at the beginning of the year, short, weekend getaways and longer weeks of rest, you will at least be forced to confront the pace of life that has crept up on you. If you must change the dates of the holiday, you will hopefully be reminded just how important the days of rest are and how much you need them. And then, you will (I hope) prioritise the rest so that you can bring your life back into a more restful rhythm again.

This may take a bit of working out. A bit of trial and error to see what works for you.

One summer, I took a week of holidays over Christmas, and then for one week in January, we hired a beach house and holidayed there together with our adult children. Those weeks were brilliant, fun, enjoyable, rejuvenating, but not very restful for the introvert in me.

In the bits and pieces in between, I intended to work. I wanted to call the time between Christmas and the 4th January 'work days'. Then from the 4th to the 11th I would be with my family, and then I'd go to work again. I took on some editing jobs and I intended to take myself to the study and do some writing. This sort of worked. The editing jobs got done. The writing didn't. I got very frustrated with myself and gave myself a few pep talks and a bit of telling off, but none of it made much difference. I realised that by trying to both work and have a holiday at the same time, I wasn't achieving either. So, I decided that I would do things differently.

The next year, I took holidays for the whole month from Christmas to my birthday (a nice easy date to remember for me). I put an out-of-office email in place. I let myself totally off the hook when it came to writing. I completely relaxed.

This resulted in, not just me, but the two of us being more rested than we have been in years. We did a lot of house maintenance and sorting. We had a few adventures and even booked in a proper week of time away from the house so that we could stop completely, without even the housework getting in the way. It was a wonderful way to start the year and it's a rhythm I hope we can stick to. We found it by trying different things.

Moz and I have also discovered that we, as a couple, work very well when we have a weekend away each quarter. And a day off each week. These are times when we stop to think, to muse, to check in on our regular pace of life and see whether anything needs changing. In between those times, life can get busy, there will be times where we push ourselves and make things happen. But if we stick to having regular breaks we will resist getting caught up in the busy-ness and rush. It is less likely that the overwhelm and struggle will be our regular way of life.

This is a good rhythm for us. I strongly recommend you find one for yourself.

Happily Ever After Syndrome

I used to think that there was a magic bullet. That there was a system or method or something that if I could just find it, just put it into place, then life would be smooth. I read a lot of Enid Blyton as a child, and I think I suffer from Happily-Ever-After syndrome.

I knew that life contained struggles. It wasn't just the Enid Blyton books – in all the novels I read the characters had serious struggles. The main character, whoever they were, had an extra tough time. But then they learned something and put it into place, and bingo! Everything was fixed and they lived happily ever after.

That's just not how life is. And I can't tell you how disappointed I am by that.

I should be able to discover a new household organising trick and then never have to clean the house again.

I should be able to figure out a particular diet and then never have to worry about putting on weight ever again.

I should be able to find an exercise routine that works and then be fit for the rest of my life.

And yes, I should be able to find a way to organise my time that means that I never have to tweak my schedule again. I will always be organised, on time, get all my tasks finished and be able to follow my dreams. (And my books should write themselves too, while we're at it.)

Life is just not like that. Things change. It doesn't take more than one small variation for your whole routine to be thrown off the rails and you feel like you have to start all over again.

This, again, is why it's helpful to think of rhythms rather than perfect systems. Balance sounds like it's a static thing, but when you watch someone balancing on a beam or one acrobat balancing another on the top of their head, you can see that balance is just one long series of corrections. Correcting this way and then that. Correction after correction after correction.

If you have put a system in place, say, one of the systems that I'm going to encourage you to use in the next section of this book, and after a few weeks or months of it working perfectly, you find that it doesn't work anymore, that's fine. That's not failure. It's not falling off the wagon. It's not 'I can't do this and I'll never get my life into line.'

What it is, is a course correction. A chance to try something new. A time to think over what worked and what didn't and to find a new way of doing things.

That's what life is like. You're not failing if you need to correct your system over and over again. What works in one year (or even in one week) won't work in the next. Your job will change, your health will change, you might have children, in which case, your life is changing all the time for the next ... well, I don't know, my eldest is 27 and she hasn't stopped changing my life yet. Or the rest of your life will change around that system until that system is no longer a perfect solution to the changed needs in your life.

Change, rhythm, balance, flow, flexibility. Keeping these ideas in mind will help you to adjust. As one activity takes more time out of your schedule, another might need to take the back seat for a while. That is just how life is.

I love the way The Message talks about learning the 'unforced rhythms of grace' from the Lord. That sounds a lot like flourishing to me, like shalom.

Activities

Take a look at your calendar. Right now, find a weekend in the next three months that you can designate a 'holiday weekend'. You don't need to go away (though I suggest you do), but choose not to put any activities, meetings, church or family commitments in that weekend. Book it, so that when anyone asks, you can say you are busy.

Take that time to assess your pace of life. Do you need to speed up? Slow down? Are you a victim of busy-creep?

PART 2: HOW

I hope at this stage that you have some idea of the kind of boots that fit you. That you have a dream that you are willing to pursue. An activity that you'd like to take the time to delight in. Or, possibly, that you have figured out that you know what your mission is and that you're already doing it (which is totally awesome) but that you need a little help putting your life together so that you can do it with more focus and give it more time.

You may be feeling totally overwhelmed as you look at what your life already holds. The nice big ideas I've been encouraging you to dream up and focus on look great from a distance, but as you look at your day tomorrow, you might have a different view altogether.

Organising your time can be like working in an overgrown garden, and believe me, I know all about overgrown gardens. (Nicely maintained gardens, I don't know so much about.) You can have a picture of what you'd like the finished project to look like, but at the moment there are so many waist-high weeds that you're not even sure that there are plants under there, and you're not sure where to start.

I am working on changing this, but at the moment, my style of gardening could best be described as 'attack gardening'. I let everything go, it gets more and more out of control, and then when Moz and I manage a spare weekend, we attack! We cut down the long grass, pull out the weeds, trim the vines, and do all the other bits and pieces. And for a little time, the garden almost looks like a garden again.

Do you feel like you are managing your life in the same way? You're not sure how to do it all, so you just wait until everything gets overwhelming and then you make a massive effort to get things done, pushing hard, working all hours, and then you drop, exhausted and feel like you've made it again.

But the roots of the problem are still there, and eventually the weeds creep up until you feel overwhelmed once again.

I hope to give you some tools in this section of the book that will allow you to not just 'attack garden' but actually garden your time. Tools that will allow regular weeding. The first section of the book has hopefully helped you to see what to plant in your time garden, and this second section will help you keep it clear so that the beautiful flowers you've planted can be a blessing to those around you.

CHAPTER TEN
The Everything List

"*Your mind is for having ideas, not holding them.*"
– David Allen

"*Before you eat the elephant, make sure you know what parts you want to eat.*"
– Todd Stocker

Write it all out

There's a tool that I use for overwhelm that works every time. It is not just recommended by me, a lot of time-management experts use this tool. It's a starting place. It's guaranteed to cut down the clutter in your head and to help you get started, even if you are completely freaking out.

It's called the Everything List.

This list requires old-school tools: a pen and a piece of paper. Or, you know, a pencil, if you want to go even older school.

Make sure the piece of paper is a big one. You can find a space to write your list in the workbook, or you can grab a piece of A4 (or larger) and go ahead using that.

This is what I want you to do:

Write down everything that you have to do on the piece of paper. Transfer everything on your mental list to the paper list.

No task is too big or too small.

Just write it all down.

- Clean the car
- Finish the report
- Make tomorrow's lunches
- Sort the sock drawer
- Paint the house
- Visit Great Aunt Mary
- Buy Christmas cards
- Write to the teacher about Billy's homework
- Take the cat to the vet

No task is too insignificant for this list. No task is too far off in the future. Every single thing that you can think of that you need to do or organise, every phone call or email you need to make, anything at all that requires an action or thought from you belongs on this list.

Resist the urge to sort the contents of this list right now. That comes later. At the moment your job is to dump all the things you've been carrying around in your head onto the piece of paper.

You might even take a couple of days or a week to complete the list. You might think of new things to put on there after you thought you were finished. That's good, just write them down.

Once you've got everything on your piece of paper you might find that you feel better already. There is a big difference between keeping it all in your head, and knowing that it's safely written down somewhere.

So enjoy that feeling. Take a few deep breaths.

Then look at the list again.

Now is the time to sort.

Things to take off the list

First, are there things on your list that are purely shoulds? Are there items that don't fit with your values? Are there tasks that are obviously not right for your personality? As you look down the list, can you see items that you can easily cross off now that you know more about where you're heading and what your goals are? Are there items that just don't fit?

Go ahead and cross those things off. See? You've simplified your life already. Well done.

Other sorting methods

There are a few ways that you can sort the remaining tasks on your list. I'll briefly outline some of them here. As you go through the list in more detail, you might find more tasks that just don't fit with how you'd like your newly examined life to be. Feel free to either cross them off or delegate them. This is a declutter of your to-do list. The simpler you can make it, the better.

1) Use your mind map

One way to sort the tasks is using the mind map you created earlier. Your mind map already divides your life into different segments. As you look at your large list, divide the tasks among the life categories. This can help you see which part of your life is the most overwhelming right now. Do you want to spend that much time and effort on that part of your life? Are the minutiae of your life crowding out the things that you want to give more attention to? Organising in this way can give you clarity.

2) Use your calendar

You can arrange the tasks according to when they need to be done. Give each task either a due date or a start date. Then add the tasks to your calendar with an alert for a reasonable reminder time.

You don't need to ring Great Aunt Mary until her birthday next month. Put it on the calendar.

Painting the house will be an autumn task, maybe next year. Put it on the calendar.

On the other hand, writing to the teacher about Billy's homework needs to be done tomorrow. So put it on your calendar for tomorrow. There will only be a (comparatively) few tasks on tomorrow's list and you can do them then.

If the task is a big one (say, painting the house) you might need to block out a lot of time for that on your calendar. If the task will take an hour, then schedule it on your calendar for an hour.

Now you don't have to think about the tasks until their due date comes around. You know your calendar will alert you when they are coming due, so you can relax and give yourself some brain space.

3) Batching

Another way of sorting your master list is to batch your tasks.

Make a list of phone calls you need to make. Things you need to do in the car. Things you need to do on the computer. Things you need to do around the house.

Or batch them under the headings of Do, Write, Call and Buy.

Then when you're in the car, do as many of those things as you can. When you're ready to make phone calls, make them all. When you are able to get into email, write as many of those pesky emails as you have time for. Do all the shopping when you are in the shopping mall.

This way you are not jumping around from one type of task to another, and once your brain is in the right kind of space, you can get all the tasks in that space done at once.

4) Important and Urgent

One method I find particularly useful when I'm feeling completely overwhelmed is the urgent/important quadrant method from Stephen Covey's *The Seven Habits of Highly Effective People*.

Divide another sheet of paper into four quadrants (you can find this in the workbook too). Along the top write the heading

Urgent on one quadrant and Not Urgent on the other, down the side in the same way write Important and Not Important.

	Urgent	Not Urgent
Important		
Not Important		

Now you divide your tasks among the quadrants. Are the tasks urgent and important (quadrant A)? Important but not urgent (quadrant B)? Not important but urgent (quadrant C)? Or neither important nor urgent (quadrant D)?

Once the tasks are sorted into the quadrants then you have four methods of dealing with them.

The A tasks are items you really need to attend to now. They can be put onto daily lists over the next week. They can be added to your calendar. Scheduling time to do the tasks – blocking out time in your calendar – is a good way to make sure they get done.

The B tasks need to be planned for in the future. However, they shouldn't just be pushed further and further away. These are still important tasks. Often they may be important to you alone.

One important but not urgent task for me is the writing of my novel. There is no one hanging over me checking that I've done my writing for the day. The writing can easily be squeezed out by other more urgent things that other people want me to do. But writing is important to me, and if I don't make the time to do it, it just won't get done. That important thing that I feel called to do will never happen.

This is why it is vital to schedule time to do the tasks in the B quadrant. While there is no urgency, the tasks are as important as the A tasks and it is up to us to make sure they get done. I set aside time every work day to work on my novel. Sometimes I have only been able to schedule 15 minutes, sometimes 30 minutes, sometimes two hours. That time needs to be held sacred. It is the time I am using to do the thing God has commissioned me to do, the thing that is important to me.

Plan for the B tasks, and put aside time each day or each week to do them. Even though they may be important only to you, they are important.

The C tasks, the urgent but not so important tasks, can be delegated to someone else. Yes, they need to be done, but they don't necessarily need to be done by you. You have things that only you can do, these tasks can be done by someone else. You might know the perfect person to do them, the person for whom they will be life-giving tasks that they will really enjoy. You might know a teenager who would really enjoy earning a bit of extra cash doing them. You might be in a position to delegate the task to an employee or to a member of your team. Either way, get them off your plate.

And the final quadrant? The not urgent, not important things? Those things should be dropped. You shouldn't be wasting your time even thinking about them. They are not important, they are not urgent, they do not need to be done. They are weeds clogging up your time garden. Pull them out and throw them away.

One last thing – make sure you keep the master list!

You might want to transfer it to a spreadsheet, or some notes software like Evernote or even to a task management app, but you really need to keep it so that your brain can relax in the knowledge that all of the tasks it was trying to remember are listed somewhere safe and sound.

Your mind is not a very good remembering machine. It remembers things at times when you can do nothing about them, and it forgets when you have the time or are in the place to actually do the task. Using a tool like the Everything List helps me clear my brain so I can spend time doing creative work while at the same time making sure I don't forget the important tasks I have to do.

Writing an Everything List is a surefire way to help you feel less overwhelmed and it is a process that can be repeated as often as you feel you need to. I don't need to write an Everything List every day or even every week, I use my calendar and my daily lists to keep on top of my everyday life and I'll talk about that more later on, but I pull the Everything List out as a tool to help me when I'm feeling like everything is getting on top of me. Overwhelm happens every now and then. It's part of the rhythm of life. It's good to have a method for dealing with it.

Activities

Write out an Everything List

Divide your list up using the Important vs Urgent quadrants

CHAPTER ELEVEN

Time budget

Parkinson's Law: Work expands so as to fill the time available for its completion.

Hofstadter's Law: It always takes longer than you expect, even when you take into account Hofstadter's Law.

Plan your time

We can't do it all. There are just too many possibilities in life. Somehow we need to drop some things. And as you are the only one living your specific life with your specific burdens and challenges and your specific energy levels, you are the one who needs to make the decisions about what your life holds.

When you look at your life and decide what you value and what you want to give more time to, you then need to take steps to make that happen. I'm sure you have some activities you want to do more, and that you have already loaded yourself with guilt about not doing them.

'I really must exercise more,' you say. Or, 'I have to spend more time just hanging out with the kids.' Or, 'I should get back in touch with my high school friends.'

Then life gets in the way and you don't.

And you won't. Not until you take concrete steps.

How do you spend your time?

The good news is that you've already taken some steps to help you put the important things into your life. This chapter is about making a time budget and the first step in any budget (time or money) is to track what you're already doing. You have already taken care of that in the mind map chapter. You might want to pull out that week of tracked time and have another look at it.

Compare your tracked time to the Important–Urgent quadrant that you made from your Everything List. How many of the activities from your tracked week belong in quadrants A (important and urgent) or B (important but not urgent)? Are you spending all your time in quadrants C and D? What can you delegate or cut out completely so that you have more time to do the things that are important to you?

Schedule in the important things

I'm sure you've heard the analogy of the rocks in the jar, but just in case, I'll go through it quickly here. The idea is that you have big rocks, small pebbles, sand and water that you would like to put into a jar. The reality is that if you put the water in first, nothing else will fit in the jar without the water flowing over the top. But, if you put the big rocks in first, then even though the jar looks full, you can still squeeze in some smaller pebbles around the big rocks. Then, even though the jar (once again) looks full, you will be able to sprinkle some of the sand into the cracks between the pebbles, and even after that, there will still be room for some water.

In this analogy, the big rocks stand for the things that are important to you. If you're not careful, these important things can be left out of your life altogether. It is very easy for your life to fill up with little unimportant things, like the jar fills up with water. You might not even notice, but when you get to the end of a week you will say, 'Oh man! I didn't make it to the gym. Again.' Or you will realise that three months have gone past and you haven't seen your really dear friends. Or you haven't practised the piano. Or, in my case, I've frittered my time away and the novel has not written itself while I wasn't looking.

We need to put the big rocks in first.

How do you do this?

You use your calendar and you schedule those big rocks in.

I've talked already about how I schedule time to write my novel. Moz and I also book in a fortnightly dinner with our son and daughter-in-law. We have a small group that meets fortnightly for fellowship and prayer. I schedule in trips to the gym.

These meetings and activities are put on my calendar. They are fixed appointments with myself and with others.

More than good intentions

I want to make it clear, good intentions are not going to cut it here. You've tried using good intentions before. You've sat in the guilt. You have a strong desire to do better. But that's not enough. You need to make actual changes in the way you think and the way you act. And you probably need support in making those changes.

Find a person, or a small group of people, that will hold you accountable. You might need someone to tell you that the important things are important. You might need their help to be able to say no to things that aren't so important. Get a support group around you, then schedule in the important things in your calendar.

Value the appointments you make with yourself. You'd hate to let a good friend down, wouldn't you? Be a good friend to yourself. If you are asked to do something else, and you look at your calendar and the time is scheduled for your non-urgent but important thing, then the time is already taken. You are not available. Apologise, (don't explain, just say 'sorry, I'm not available') and try to find another time for the request.

You can't do everything

Here's the crunch. You will not be able to fit everything into your day or your week. There is always more to do than you will have time for. You need to budget your time so that you know what you have time to take part in, and which activities you will have to decline. You need to know what your limits and boundaries are.

Here's an example from my life: I like to have coffee with people. Coffee, tea, hot chocolate, it doesn't matter what you drink, but the time together with my friends for decent one-to-one conversation is very important to me. But I have realised that I can't just have coffee with someone every time I'm asked, or even every time I want to. I have other important tasks to do too.

So I have budgeted my coffee time. I can fit two coffees with people in each week. Once I have filled up those coffee slots, they are full. They might not occur at the same time for every friend, but once I have two meet ups with friends in a week, then I have reached my budget.

Another part of my life involves leading (or MCing) church services. I really enjoy doing that, but I've decided that in my time budget I can only lead one service a month. Sometimes, if it's a busier season, I will only allow two services every three months. Whatever I choose, it is good to be clear so that when I am asked, I can give a direct answer about my availability.

When you make a money budget, you need to decide how much to give, how much to save and how much to spend. With a time budget it is the same. How much time will you give away, by having coffee with people, or serving at church? How much time will you spend on your important tasks? How much on the urgent tasks? And how much will you save?

When I talk about saving time in the context of a time budget, I am really talking about resting. Taking time out for relaxation and for holidays is actually a time saver, as it helps your brain to feel rested and renewed. Resting is also essential for your brain to be able to make creative connections. Therefore, when you get back to your regular work, you will work better, often faster, and definitely more creatively. Rest is so important that I've given it its own chapter where you can read more.

Clear and unambiguous answers

A time budget helps you to be clear in your communication. If someone asks you to do something you can say 'yes' or 'no' in a timely manner. This either tells them that the task is now taken care of, or it gives them plenty of time to find someone else to do whatever needs doing.

Without a time budget, I tend to put off answering people who ask me to do things. 'Are you available on March 23rd?' they ask. I don't know. I don't know what that week holds. Will I be flat out? Or will I be relatively relaxed? I can't see that far into the future so I don't answer straight away. I think I'll know much better what my week holds when it comes closer to the time, so I put off my response. Then, when it really comes to the crunch, no matter how busy I am, I always say 'yes'. Why? Because I know I haven't left them enough time to find another volunteer.

It is much better for me to have a pre-made time budget. If I know there is time free in that section of the budget (time put aside for volunteer work, or time put aside to meet with people) then I can say yes. After that, I will say no to any other requests for that week. However, if that time is already booked then I can say 'no' as early as possible, so that another person can be found to do whatever it is that needs doing. I shouldn't feel an obligation to say yes every time. Sometimes it is better for someone other than me to be given the opportunity to do the task. A time budget helps me to know what my answer is.

The planning fallacy

There is a problem that occurs when you start making a time budget, and that is something called 'the planning fallacy'.[32] We tend to underestimate how much time a task takes to get done. We are optimistic. We think things will be better this time around – we'll work faster, be more efficient. Or we don't think clearly about the time that it takes to do a task.

For example, when I put the task of leading at church into my time budget, I might think that this task will only take up the Sunday morning. That is when church is, and that's when I'm leading. But in reality, leading church takes much more time than that. I need to put aside the time to think and pray about the service, I need to write up a running sheet, I must take the time to check whether the readers are ready and whether or not the person praying has decided to include The Lord's Prayer, I need to know that the children's talk is good to go, and to ask the music leader what songs we will be singing. I may even need to put aside time to ring around various people and ask them to volunteer for other aspects of the service. This can take up to another two hours in the week before the service.

When I'm checking my time budget to see if I can be involved in this way, I need to think about all that the job involves, not just the little bit at the end.

A meeting in town requires travel to and from the meeting place, it requires reading through the associated paperwork, it requires preparation time. This needs to be added in when putting the meeting into your calendar. Or even when thinking about whether you can go in the first place.

---

[32]Pezzo, Mark V.; Litman, Jordan A.; Pezzo, Stephanie P. (2006). "On the distinction between yuppies and hippies: Individual differences in prediction biases for planning future tasks". Personality and Individual Differences. **41** (7): 1359–1371.

Kahneman, Daniel; Tversky, Amos (1982). "Intuitive prediction: Biases and corrective procedures". In Kahneman, Daniel; Slovic, Paul; Tversky, Amos (eds.). Judgment Under Uncertainty: Heuristics and Biases. Science. Vol. 185. pp. 414–421.

Writing a report requires time for research, time to collate information, and possibly time to talk with the other stakeholders, as well as the time for writing. And then the actual writing of the report will also probably take longer than you thought it would in the first place.

The planning fallacy also applies to bigger tasks such as preparing taxes or completing an assignment. I might clearly know how long it took to do my taxes last year, but might be confident (for no good reason) that this year will be different. Or I might see how long it takes others to do a job, but decide that it will take me less time than them, even though there is no evidence for such a thing.

Keep track

One way that you can combat your planning fallacy issues is by tracking time, just like we talked about in the 'Chapter Three' chapter. When I started tracking my time, I realised that a half-hour jog at the gym takes me about one hour and five minutes to complete. That's how long it takes to get changed, drive to the gym, do the jog, stretch, drive home, and get changed out of my gym gear ready to get back to work. It would be tempting to think that a half-hour jog would take, I don't know, half an hour? Or at worst 45 minutes. But for me it takes just over an hour, and more if I shower, so I need to allow that much time in my time budget for exercise each day.

Timing the activities in the day helps to bring clarity and truth to our days. We will no longer be guessing how long it takes to unload the dishwasher or check our email, we will know.

Another method for overcoming the planning fallacy is to make implementation intentions[33] – that is, concrete plans that show how, when and where you will act on a task. This gives you more focus on the task, you allow fewer interruptions, and you are much more likely to get the task done in the amount of time you set for it. This also helps with Parkinson's Law – the understanding that the work will expand to take up the time you have to spend on it.

A third possible help is to cut larger tasks into smaller pieces and allocate time to each of the individual tasks. This takes a bit of thinking, but it helps you to be more accurate about the time that a large task will take.

Think before answering

I love to help people out. I really enjoy the feeling of saying 'yes, I can do that' and most of the time I also enjoy the feeling of doing the thing and helping the person. It is so tempting, when asked to help out, to just imagine the calendar (instead of actually looking at it), and to make the other person feel wonderful by saying, 'Certainly. I'll help. Tell me what to do.' But this has led me into some truly awful situations where I have loaded my plate with altogether too much work, and I have had to let my friends down at the last minute as I can't actually do what they've asked me to.

To avoid this, I need to take the time to think before I answer. I need to hear the request, really think about all that it will entail (perhaps even thinking about it over a couple of days) and then only say 'yes' when I know that the task fits within my time budget and also matches with my values and important tasks.

---

[33]Koole, Sander; Van't Spijker, Mascha (2000). "Overcoming the planning fallacy through willpower: Effects of implementation intentions on actual and predicted task-completion times". European Journal of Social Psychology. **30** (6): 873–888

One in, one out

The other day I was asked whether I would like to be part of a very exciting opportunity. I was thrilled to be asked, but my answer was, 'I'll pray about it.' That is one very good way to give yourself time to think before answering.

I was talking with my mother about the opportunity, and she asked me a very good question.

'What are you going to give up?' she asked.

She knows that my schedule is full, that I already have many projects that I enjoy that I am making time for. She cut through my excitement about helping my friend with that simple question. In order to put something new into my time I will need to cut something out. I can't just pile more and more on my plate. If I do, something will fall off the edge and it will likely be something very important, like family relationships, peace, or sleep. In order to take on something new, I need to cut something else out. In order to put something into my schedule, I need to pull something else out.

It's like putting new clothes into a full closet. If I buy a new shirt, then an old shirt has to be either trashed or donated.

I'm still deciding whether to take on this new opportunity. But now I'm also thinking about what I will give up, in order to take on something new.

Thanks, Mum.

Askers vs guessers

When I am asked a favour, I always assume that the person who is asking me has thought through all the possibilities when it comes to the perfect person for the task, and they've decided that I'm the only one who will be able to do it. I'm the one, the chosen one. I'm the person out of all their friends who is the least busy, or the most suited to the job, or who has the best spare room where their Aunt Frederika can stay for four weeks because it's closest to all of the shops and amenities.

This may not be the case. I may be nothing special, just one of the five or ten people they will ask until one finally says, 'yes'.

Jocelyn K. Glei divides people up into 'askers' and 'guessers'.[34] Guessers, like me, will think hard about who the best person is to ask to do a certain task. They look at the other person's life, or what they know of it, and they will only ask for a favour if they think the other person will say 'yes'.

Askers, on the other hand, will just ask. They will ask and keep on asking until they find a person to do a task. They will ask, expecting you to say 'no' if the request is unreasonable or if it is just not convenient.

It can be very freeing to think that you are not expected to answer every request with a 'yes'. Sometimes, the asker might be just as happy if you say 'no'. They just want an answer.

You will have an answer if you've spent a little time putting a time budget together. You will know whether you have the time to give, or whether you need to spend more time on your important tasks and can't take any out for another non-important thing, no matter how urgent.

Life on purpose

Let's live our lives as if we're living on purpose. Let's not fall into saying 'yes' to every little request that's made of us. Let's not fill up our lives with unimportant but urgent tasks that

---

[34]Jocyeln K Glei, *Unsubscribe: How to Kill Email Anxiety*

don't get us any closer to our dream, or don't allow us to live out the life God has planned for us.

Let's budget the big things in, and schedule the time to do them. The sand and water will take care of themselves.

Activities

Refer to your time tracker, or track another week of your time. Use the knowledge of your time use to inform a time budget.

Schedule time on your calendar for the important tasks in your time budget, and write an implementation intention:

I will [behaviour] at [time] in [location]

CHAPTER TWELVE

Rest

"*Come to me, all you who are weary and burdened, and I will give you rest.*"
– Jesus (Matthew 11:28, NIV)

"*When you rest, you catch your breath and it holds you up, like water wings …*"
– Anne Lamott

Not a reward, an essential

I've been promising this chapter for a long time. Rest is such an important subject that it has crept into many of the other chapters that I've written. It's such an important subject that there have been multiple books written about it. I'll suggest a few at the end of this chapter, but one person who has collated a lot of scientific information about the effects and necessity for rest is Alex Soojung-Kim Pang. His book is called *Rest: Why You Get More Done When You Work Less*, and I highly recommend it.

Attitudes towards rest seem to be changing, which I think is a good thing. Look at any courtroom or medical drama from the 1990s (yes, I'm that old) and you will see that the people we were supposed to look up to, the ones saving lives or keeping innocent people out of gaol and prosecuting the guilty, were doing all that on three hours of sleep. They would stay up all night working, then drink a large coffee, and take the life of someone in their hands. Successfully, for the most part, but this was TV after all.

I don't know about you, but I don't really want someone doing brain surgery on me after having worked 48 hours straight. Not when I know that lack of sleep has a similar effect to a blood alcohol reading that would get you arrested in Australia if you tried to drive.[35] I definitely wouldn't want a drunk surgeon, and the performance impairment is pretty much the same.

Sleep is vitally important, and so is the time to creatively rejuvenate. Basically, as well as working, we also need rest

---

[35]https://www.cdc.gov/niosh/work-hour-training-for-nurses/longhours/mod3/08.html

and play. All these things are important to our wellbeing as humans.

Rest as a reward?

My brain tells me that if I get all my tasks done, then I can rest. I guess that worked well when I was a child. In primary school, the tasks that I needed to do were limited. I could finish my homework, practise the piano, make my bed and put my clothes away, then I could read, or go play outside, or watch TV. Work first, then play. Makes sense, right?

But now, as an adult, I struggle, because the tasks are never done. I might have vacuumed the house, made dinner, and finished all the washing, but I could still clean the windows, declutter a cupboard or go out and weed the garden. Even in my work life, the work is never-ending. I might write a chapter of this book, but then I could edit it, I could write another chapter, I could do some marketing, I could clean up my office, I could brainstorm for the next book.

If I wait for my work to be done before I rest, then I will never rest. The work is never done.

That's not to say that your life should be all rest and no work. There needs to be a balance of both. But if you're reading this book, I reckon that your balance is skewed towards work. I wonder how long it has been since you undertook an activity just for the joy of it? How hard was it for you to write up the list of things you enjoy doing, back in the personality chapter?

Rest is something we need to build into our lives. Something we need to book in first.

Sabbath

This is my starting point. A day of rest each week. A day of recreation, rejuvenation, delight.

I have compared time to money before. I'm going to do it again. When I put together my budget, when I look at how I'm going to spend my money, one of the first things I do is separate 10% to give away. It's called a tithe, and I take that out of the pot of money first. We started doing this as a family when Moz and I were studying at university and living on government payments. We were not wealthy by any means. As a family of four, we learned to make everything stretch. One friend said that it was, 'bread and butter but no jam' and that's a good explanation.

However, we learned that if we put aside 10% of our funds to give away, somehow the rest of the money covered the expenses that arrived. Sometimes we even had little miracles, like the cheque that arrived in our mailbox one day, that paid for the bill that had arrived the day before, right down to the last five cents.

Giving 10% away first is an act of faith. We do it in faith that God will provide what we need (note, what we need, not necessarily what we want) afterwards. If, during that financially stretchy time, we had waited until the end of the week and given away the money that was left in our pay cheque, there would have been no money to give away. We had to put that 10% away first, and then use the rest for the expenses that came our way.

For me, taking a sabbath is exactly the same. It is time that I put aside to rest in an act of faith that God will give me the time and energy in the rest of the week to do what he has called me to do. Maybe not all that I want to do, but all that is necessary.

If I don't take a sabbath each week, I start to feel as if getting the work done totally depends on me. I feel like the work rests on my shoulders and if I don't work like a maniac to get it all done, then some major catastrophe will happen. I get wound up. I start working faster and faster, with more and more anxiety. Not that I'm getting more done, you understand. The faster work leads to more mistakes and more of the work needs to be done over, leading to it all taking more time. I become like a tightly wound spring. I can't relax to chat with anyone, I can't enjoy my family, I must work, harder and longer. Not only seven days a week, but in the evenings as well. And I become very, very tired.

However, if I take a sabbath, I unwind. It might take most of the day, depending on how stressful work has been that week, but eventually my shoulders relax, I lose the permanent wrinkle on my brow, my jaw unclenches. I can smile and laugh and enjoy conversation and the results last well into the next week.

It's a circuit breaker. It's fantastic. I highly recommend it.

So, what do I mean by a sabbath?

Firstly, a sabbath is a day that you take once a week for rest. It doesn't have to be a Sunday. (Ask your pastor just how restful her or his Sunday is.) But it is best to keep the same day each week. This helps you to prepare for it and to relax into it.

I mostly take a sabbath on a Saturday. If some unavoidable activity occurs on the Saturday, then I will switch to the Sunday and (gasp!) take a break from church that day. But mostly Saturdays are my day of blissful relaxation.

I read books – fun novels, or deep spiritual tomes, whatever I'm in the mood for. I listen to audiobooks so that I can knit while I'm 'reading'. I go for coffee or brunch with Moz. I go for a leisurely walk. I might watch a murder mystery. I nap. I deeply relax. That's what my sabbath looks like.

But this day of rest will look different for you than it does for me. And also, it will change for you (and me) from week to week, depending on your needs and circumstances. I don't have many hard and fast rules. I believe that the sabbath should be a day of rest, so Rule 1 is that there is no work on that day. But what is work? I reckon it is different for each of us.

I used to say that gardening was work for me, and that it's restful for others. Maybe it's because I'm in mid-life now, but I'm beginning to enjoy gardening. I'm finding this hard to believe even as I write it! Even though there are spiders hiding in those weeds, and it's hard physical work, gardening is something creative and different from the sitting in front of a computer that I do Monday to Friday. So now I allow myself some gardening on my sabbath. But only if I desire to do it, not if it feels like an obligation.

I don't do any writing on my sabbath now, though back when I was working at a university, creative writing was the thing that I spent my sabbath doing. Now writing is my nine-to-five work, which is a complete privilege. But it does mean that now I don't do writing on the sabbath. And definitely no email!

Work and play

I suggest that you write down a list of things that look like work to you. And then take one day a week when you don't do those things.

I also suggest that you write a list of things that look like rest or play. Things like reading, going for a bushwalk with your family, playing a board game, going out for coffee, attending a concert. These are the things to do on your day off.

Some people like to avoid anything to do with commerce on their sabbath. Others like to go out for a special meal at a café. Some like to cook double the day before so that they don't have to be in the kitchen at all on the sabbath, others like to cook special meals that have meaning for them and their family on the sabbath day. There is no one-size-fits-all here. Your idea of rest and mine will be different.

One thing though, it's a good idea to limit screen time on this day. Screens can be deceptive. You can feel like you're relaxing, but a day spent in front of a TV or scrolling through social media can leave you more drained than you were when you started. Some who write on this subject call for a complete screen detox once a week, and I'm not going that far (because I haven't gone without the phone for the whole day myself) but I believe that limiting your screen time will make the day more restful and much more energising.

Good books that helped me define my sabbath are *Invitation to Solitude and Silence* by Ruth Haley Barton and *Spacemaker* by Daniel Sih. Both these authors have built a sabbath into their lives, but they've done it in very different ways and I found the comparison of the two gave me balance when I designed my own sabbath.

Taking a day off each week, giving that time to God, delighting in his creation and his re-creation of you, is a gift from him, it's a joy, it's life-giving. At the very least, it's worth a try.

Holidays

One day off each week is the bare minimum of rest that's needed. The next thing I want to suggest is holidays. I remember being told by a good friend that a life of rest should involve one day off a week, one weekend a quarter, and four weeks a year. I reckon this balance is about right.

The thing about holidays is that you can get so busy working that a whole year slips away without you noticing. Suddenly, your human resources department is telling you that your annual leave has built up, and you realise that five years have gone by without you having a decent break.

It's so easy to miss holidays, so tempting to just keep working. But these long breaks are where your brain does the creative work in the background. This is where you get those leaps of intuition that make your work life so much more valuable. This, to use the budget analogy, is the equivalent of saving money. This is where you *save time*.

It was during his holidays that Bill Gates figured out the importance of the internet. It was on a walk along a river that Ernö Rubik came up with the Rubik's cube. Sometimes you don't come up with your creative solutions or ideas on the actual holiday, but the connection might show up afterwards. However, many of these creative ideas can be traced back to the time spent resting and recreating, even if they actually pop into your mind once you get back to your desk.

So how do you make sure that you get the holidays you need? You book them in *first*. Sit down with your calendar, decide when you're taking time off, and book it in.

Now, this might take a bit of practice. But even if you have to change your weekend off from *this* weekend to *that* one because something has come up in the meantime that you simply cannot miss, you are still prioritising your rest, and the act of changing your rest day on your calendar will bring it to mind for you. There is a far greater chance of you getting the rest you need if you put aside the time for it. Rest and holidays are some of the big rocks that need to be put in first.

Remember, this is not wasted time. This is saved time. This time off will allow you to work with greater focus and purpose when you get back to work. It will allow you to be more relaxed and generous with the people in your life because you've filled your own energy tank. This is not selfish. It is self care. It will allow you to give out more in the balance of the year without feeling burnt out and exhausted.

Book your holidays in. First.

Silence and solitude

This spiritual discipline, just like the sabbath, is a gift straight from heaven.

You might not think so. You might be terrified of spending any time in silence. But I'm here to tell you that my daily time of silence and solitude is one of the greatest things that my life now holds.

Spending time with our own thoughts is not a popular pastime these days. One of my friends decided that she needed a massage. When she got back, she told me that she thought they should install small TVs under the massage table so that you don't need to just lie there and listen to your thoughts. I can't think of much that would be less relaxing.

But we all carry a small TV in our pockets these days. A small distraction device. And we use it any time we get the slightest bit bored. Standing in line at the checkout? Pull out your phone and start scrolling. Waiting for the bus? Start scrolling. Sitting in the café waiting for your coffee? More scrolling.

Those little waiting times used to be unintentional mindfulness moments for us. Maybe in your youth you called it 'boredom'. But whether you were bored, or whether you noticed the little butterfly wandering past or the breeze on your face or the background chatter of the café, you had the time in those moments to get a little more in touch with yourself and how you were feeling. These days, you're more likely to find a little something to be amused (or outraged) by on your phone. Distracting ourselves has become a habit, and it's a very difficult one to break.

I have not broken this habit. I tend to automatically start a podcast on my phone whenever I have more than a 30-second break to fill. I tend to avoid mindfulness.

There's another problem too. As I go through my day, I can feel more and more wound up. I have a list of tasks that need doing, and more tasks add themselves to my list as I go on. The stress builds. Will I get it all done? I've talked about the sabbath being a circuit breaker in a week of being wound up. But is there something that I can do to stop the daily anxiety treadmill?

I can wake up in the morning already feeling the stress of all the tasks I put on my list the day before. Even if there are not external deadlines or tasks to be done for clients, I can still put myself under pressure to be what my psych calls 'Christianly productive'. I need to be doing something, something that will benefit others, all the time.

So I'm distracting myself, or I'm working. There seems to be no other option.

But there is another option, and it's a good one. It is silence and solitude.

I'm not talking a month-long silent retreat here (though some days that sounds blissful). I am just talking about a little pocket of the day where I sit in silence, all by myself.

Do you look at those photos on the socials of people sitting at a table with a cup of steaming coffee, just staring out into the beauty outside, and sigh and think, 'I'd just love that.' Just rest. Just for a few moments.

That is what my silence and solitude is like.

Yes, it's a discipline. Yes, I need to schedule it into my day. But it is such a joy, a circuit breaker from the work, and a chance to check in with myself and with God and see how we really are doing today. I highly recommend it.

This is how I do it:

I set my phone to 'do not disturb' and usually leave it in another room, just so I'm not tempted to pick it up. Before I start my silent time, I write a list of all the things that I am anxious about that day. Sometimes the list is a page long, sometimes it is two or three items. I give that list to God, asking him to take care of those things. I choose not to ruminate on them in my silent time. If they come into my mind during the time, I give them back to God and choose to think on something else.

I set a timer for 15 minutes. I sit in a special place in the sunshine. Sometimes with a coffee, sometimes without. I might say The Lord's Prayer. But mostly I just sit. I focus on my breathing. Is it nice deep breathing? Or is it small shallow breaths? Is my tummy tight and roiling, or is it relaxed? Are my shoulders tight? Am I clenching my jaw? I consciously relax and breathe deeply.

I listen. Are there birds singing outside? Are there any other noises?

Is there something that keeps coming back into my mind? Sometimes I write it down. Other times I let it go, focus back on my breathing, relax my muscles.

I do that for 15 minutes. Then my timer goes off. I head into the day relaxed, re-energised and more in touch with myself and God.

If sitting still is not your thing, you can have the same experience by going for a walk, or a ride, or even a swim. The main thing is to leave your phone alone. Look at what is around you. What can you see? What can you hear? Check in with your body. What are you feeling? What is tight? Are you relaxed? Be curious, do not be judgemental.

When you hear the words 'silence and solitude' or even the words 'spiritual discipline' you can feel scared. Like this is a load on your shoulders. Another 'should' that you have to squeeze into your day. But I have found that a short time of silence and solitude each day takes the load off my shoulders. It helps me to realise (like the sabbath does) that the world will continue to circle the sun even if I don't keep up with my stuff. That life doesn't all depend on me.

Fifteen minutes a day is a small sacrifice to make for that peace of mind, for that inner rest that brings peace into everything else I do that day.

I encourage you to try it. Find a few minutes each day to sit or walk in silence. Just you and God. It's a gift.

Sleep

I don't know if you've noticed, but napping is a thing in the Bible. Jesus napped on the boat in the storm.[36] Jacob slept with his head on a rock.[37] When Elijah was feeling totally overwhelmed, God told him to sleep and eat.[38] While we are encouraged in Proverbs not to let this get out of control,[39] in the Psalms we are told that sleep is a gift from the Lord.[40]

Most adults need between seven and eight hours of sleep a night. When we sleep, our brain cells actually shrink, and a cleansing fluid sweeps through to wash away dangerous plaques and toxins.[41]

---

[36]Matthew 8

[37]Genesis 28

[38]1 Kings 19

[39]Proverbs 20:13

[40]Psalm 127:2

[41]https://www.health.harvard.edu/mind-and-mood/are-toxins-flushed-out-of-the-brain-during-sleep

I think it's important that we prioritise sleep. And I always have. I love my sleep, the more the better.

Moz hasn't always prioritised sleep. He worked out that he needed to sleep for about seven hours to feel energised each day, and he used to stay up each evening, noodling about on the computer, until about seven hours before the alarm would go off the next morning. Then he would finally come to bed and try to fall asleep immediately. This practice led to some stress. If he didn't fall asleep immediately then he would worry about how he was missing sleep, and that would lead to more stress and less sleep.

Eventually, he got sick of the stress and poor sleep and decided to go to bed earlier. Just an hour or so earlier. Most days that meant that he would wake up about an hour or so before the alarm went off in the morning. Then he would get up and noodle about on the computer until it was time to bring me a coffee in bed and start the day (yes, I am one of the world's most blessed women). He would get the same amount of computer noodling time, but there would be a lot less stress, and if he needed to catch up on sleep, there was time available to do it.

There are a few tried and true methods for getting enough sleep. Firstly, make sure your bedroom is used only for sleep and bed-related activities. No working on your laptop in bed. Your brain needs to know that the bedroom is where you go to sleep. Keep your phone in another room. People will get the idea that you're not contactable until morning. This is how it used to be, and this is how it can be again. If you need an alarm in the morning, buy yourself an alarm clock that you can put beside your bed.

Blue light from phones or screens tends to wake your brain up. It gives your neurons the impression that it's early morning, wake-up time. So turn your screens off about an hour before bedtime.

The other benefit of turning off your screens is that you're not surfing social media and filling your mind with outrage and tension from what you read there. There's not much that's more effective than outrage to stop you from heading into a deep relaxing sleep. Using your imagination by reading a book is much more likely to get you into the mood for drifting off and dreaming. Reading is always a good idea if you ask me.

Avoid caffeinated drinks after midday. Or, you know, avoid them altogether. I'll tell you a secret: If you cut right down on caffeine as a normal thing, then you get an amazing buzz from the cup of coffee that you drink when you really need one. Also, you can feel like you're on holidays if you cut caffeine from your life. Things just naturally feel less fraught and more relaxed.

I know that I am very sensitive to caffeine, and I have had seasons where I need to cut it out from my diet completely. Other times, up to two or three coffees a day has been fine. Listen to your body, it will tell you what you need. If you find yourself buzzing and unable to sit still in your silence and solitude time, it may be a sign that you need to cut out a coffee or two.

Keep your bedroom fairly cool. This helps your body cool down, which is what it naturally wants to do when you're sleeping.

Store a little notebook and a pen near your bed. If you wake up with worries or if you remember a task you need to do the next day, jot it down in your notebook, then relax. You won't forget. It's written down. (This needs to be a notebook and not a phone because of the blue-screen issue.)

Another thing that helps with sleep is, of course, exercise. Thirty minutes spent walking, riding, running, or just intentionally moving your body in some way will contribute to a good night's sleep.

These are not magic spells, and there may still be nights where sleep doesn't come easily to you. You may find that a herbal supplement helps to train your body to relax, or that you need a little more help from your doctor or a therapist. However you do it, prioritising sleep will help you to feel energetic and to think clearly as you attempt your tasks each day. And that's what we all want.

Our bodies are not meant to work like machines. We can go without food for quite some time, but if we try to go without sleep, things fall over very quickly. Part of a balanced life is the time we take for rest, for fun and for sleep. These are not rewards for work well done, these are things we are made for.

This may all sound a little idealistic to you, but I encourage you to look out for times when you can take a break, to prioritise sleep, and to entrust your work to God, knowing that he can look after it while you rest.

Activities

Open up your calendar and book in two weeks of holidays sometime in the next 12 months. Contact your human resources department or talk to your spouse or book a flight or ask a friend if you can use their beach house. Make it a real commitment. A holiday to look forward to.

Read some good books about rest and spiritual practices. I suggest

Margin, Restoring Emotional Physical Financial and Time Reserves to Overloaded Lives – Richard Swenson

Rest: Why You Get More Done When You Work Less – Alex Soojung-Kim Pang

Invitation to Solitude and Silence – Ruth Haley Barton

Spacemaker: How to Unplug, Unwind & Think Clearly in the Digital Age – Daniel Sih

CHAPTER THIRTEEN

Day-to-day strategies

"A schedule defends from chaos and whim. It is a net for catching days. It is a scaffolding on which a worker can stand and labor with both hands at sections of time."
– Annie Dillard

"Decluttering Question #1: If I needed this item, where would I look for it first? Take it there now.
Decluttering Question #2: If I needed this item, would it ever occur to me that I already had one?"
– Dana K. White

General organisation

What do you do when you have an idea? You're sitting on the bus and suddenly the most brilliant design for a can opener that actually opens cans and won't slice your fingers off comes into your mind. What do you do?

What do you do when someone asks, 'Can we meet for coffee Tuesday next week?'

When you need to pack for a weekend away, how do you know what to pack?

How do you remember what you need to buy at the grocery store?

How do you remember where your child's reader is? And do you know when it's due back at school?

Do you keep all these various thoughts in your head, hoping that the thing you need to remember – say, that you need cakes for the bake sale – pops to the front of all the other things at an appropriate time, and not at 2 a.m. the day before the cake sale. Or worse, never at all?

When my children were in primary school, one of the mothers realised that she would never be able to remember which day was sports day, which was library day, and which was the special day when her children had to bring that super-important craft thing they'd been working on for two weeks. She had a special way of getting around that problem. She used a friend.

She would ring up her friend to check, 'Sports uniform today? Great.' And her kids got through school without too much major embarrassment. I'm not sure what methods her friend used to remember all the things.

It would be good to have a personal assistant on call at all times to help us remember all the different things that our lives hold, but for most of us, that's not the way it works.

If I want to fulfil my purpose, have time to follow my dream, and use my unique gifting to serve others, I don't want to waste my time each day looking for my keys, or taking that third trip to the store for the things I didn't remember to buy the other two times. And I definitely don't want to forget my creative ideas or solutions to problems.

In this chapter I'm going to give you some strategies that I use day-to-day to keep my life working efficiently and effectively.

I'm going to take you through a few different places and times when things need to be remembered. I'll let you know what I do, and some different ways of dealing with each situation. There are many options, and you'll probably think of more as I go through. The main aim is to have a limited number of places where you keep things that you need to remember, so that you can find the thing or the memory when it is appropriate to do so, but don't have to keep it in your mind through all the inappropriate times. I call these places 'brain buckets'. I limit the number of buckets that I keep things in, so that I limit the amount of time spent searching for those things and can focus on the activities that are most important to me.

Groceries

I use a grocery app that syncs with Moz's phone so that we both can add groceries to the list as we see them running out. You empty out the teabag box? You pull out your phone and put teabags on the grocery list. Then the next time you go to the store, you don't have to stand in front of the whole shelf of hot drink possibilities trying to visualise your pantry, you can just check the list and see whether teabags are on it.

If you don't want to use an app on your phone for this purpose, I find that a paper list stuck to the fridge with a magnet works almost as well. And that has has the added bonus that people sometimes write you nice notes on the paper list. However, a magnetised pen that hangs next to the paper list is absolutely essential for the paper list to work well. Adding things to the list needs to be easy, or you will not do it.

I like the app better, purely because if I'm out and think of something I would like to buy or make, I can whip out my phone and add the groceries right there and then without having to try to remember once I get home.

Creative thoughts and ideas

I have a little notebook that I keep in my handbag. I also keep a couple of pens in there. If you're male, your pockets are probably big enough to hold a little notebook and a couple of pens without any need for an extra handbag. Girl pockets are getting larger, but the fashion industry still has a way to go in this area.

I use the notebook for creative thoughts that might strike me in the middle of the sermon at church, or as I go for a walk along the beach, or when I'm chatting with someone. As soon as it seems polite, I put the idea in the notebook. Then it is there when I want it again.

I have a similar notebook next to my bed. I don't bring my phone to the bedroom (see the Chapter Twelve chapter) but I need a place to note ideas or worries or to-do lists so that they stop nagging at me when I'm trying to sleep. I jot them down in the book, and transfer them to a more appropriate place the next day.

I also keep a dream journal next to my bed. When I'm writing creatively, my dreams become quite interesting and I write them down as soon as I wake up, while I remember them. They have turned into great short stories and have added to my novels. I keep them all together in the dream journal.

Packing lists

I used to go on holidays, get to the place we were going, unpack and then think about all the things we had forgotten. Like the HDMI cable so that we could watch movies on the larger screen, or the fan so that Moz could be cool and comfortable at night, or the rubber gloves so that I could wash up in nice hot soapy water without drying out my skin. These are all things that I had forgotten once, and would forget again.

But I found a method that helped. It is a packing list. I keep it on my phone and it syncs to my computer using the Evernote app. Anytime I go anywhere, packing is now amazingly easy because everything I have to remember, from hiking boots to dark chocolate, is written on my packing list. I no longer need to remember, I only need to check the list.

This has also made packing much faster. I used to begin packing weeks before the outing, putting random things in my case as I remembered them in the hope that I would eventually remember all the things I needed. I changed my strategy, from packing the items to writing them on a list so that I would remember the things when packing time actually came. Then it struck me that these lists I was writing before each trip were 95% identical and that if I kept one reusable list I would be set. Now it takes me about half an hour to pack and I'm very comfortable that I will have everything I need.

Daily lists and master lists

This is another area where I've gone through a few iterations to see what works best for me. I have tried using the Evernote app to keep my Everything List (transcribing it there after I'd written it out by hand) and then writing out daily lists in the app, but I found I would forget to look at the app, so I would forget to do things. Also, electronically deleting tasks off the

Everything List didn't hit my dopamine button. An empty document doesn't look nearly as satisfying as a page of tasks with everything crossed off.

I also tried using an app called Actions. I still have this app on my phone, and when I need to remember a task, and I'm not at home to use my regular daily list, I'll pop it on Actions with a date, time, and reminder so that when I am back at home I will be reminded to do the thing. I don't generally look at this list, as a rule. But if you're the kind of person that will check a list on your phone through the day, then go for it!

Right now, I am back to using a simple notebook for my lists. I am writing a large list, once a week. This is my master list. On it I write tasks that can't be scheduled and need to be done at some stage, as well as the things that need to be done in the week ahead.

Then, each day I write a smaller list. I transfer onto the daily list the things from the master list that must be done that day. The daily list needs to be small. I generally use 1/4 to 1/3 of an A5 page. Or if I use a page-to-a-week A5 diary, the daily entry space is ideal for a daily list. I know of one person who uses Post-It notes (I think they are the 7.5 cm x 12.5 cm size) to write the list. It is good to limit the size of this list because you only want to put on it the things you can do in a day. If the task doesn't fit in the small available space, it doesn't fit in your day. Move it to the next day's entry.

Calendar

I have found an electronic calendar to be one of the most helpful tools I use to organise my life. I use it to keep track of appointments, bills that need to be paid (I schedule them for a couple of days before the bill is due, just in case), recurring activities, and things that are happening that I need to know about but don't actually need to do anything about.

In my calendar this week I have a doctor's appointment, a meeting with a pastor at church, a walk with a friend, and the regular dinner and coffee time that I have with my parents. I have a bill I need to pay on Wednesday, and a reminder to put the roast in the oven earlier in the day so that we are not waiting until 8 p.m. to eat.

I have also scheduled a time to record my podcast (A Quiet Life). I don't generally do this, it's usually something that just goes on my daily and weekly list, but this week I found that the days were getting quite full, and to make sure that I actually recorded the podcast, I reserved time for it on my calendar.

My uncle's birthday is a recurring reminder that falls in this week (he's not on Facebook, so I don't get reminded that way) and there's also an entry to show when my aunt heads back to Queensland after her visit here to Tasmania. I don't really need to do much about those, especially the latter – we're not expected to take her to the airport or anything – but they are just good things to know.

I find the calendar extremely helpful when working out my time budget. I can look at the week and instantly see how many times I have booked in coffee with a friend, and how much time is taken up by extras like doctors appointments. That helps me to set my expectations and to be able to say 'yes' or 'no' to whatever opportunities come my way.

The other wonderful thing about my electronic calendar is that it has a 'family' option. So now I don't need to keep nagging Moz or reminding him of activities that we are doing together. I put it on the calendar, and the calendar does all the nagging for me. That's outsourcing!

The entries in your calendar don't necessarily need to make sense to anyone else, they just need to make sense to you. Before he left home, our son used to be a part of our family calendar. He still gets email reminders of our family activities. He had to get in touch one time and ask what the entry was that said, 'Yelling in church'. There was also a 'practice yelling in church' entry. These were days when Moz was a villager in our church children's Christmas play. I'm not sure that many people have booked 'yelling in church' into their calendar, but it worked for us.

The calendar is a tool, not a boss. Don't let your calendar boss you around, but do use it to remind you of things you need to remember on a given date, and to help you schedule your time.

One more thing on calendars: As far as you can, don't schedule meetings back to back. I don't know your work situation, but I'm very rarely in a place where I can walk out of a meeting, across the hallway, and into the next meeting straight away. I always have travel time between meetings. And as well as travel time, there could also be significant parking time. Take these things into account when you schedule your time.

If the traffic is miraculously clear and you find a parking spot directly outside the place you need to go, and therefore you have five or ten extra minutes before the meeting, that's fine. Use that time as mindful thinking time, or write some notes in that notebook you carry, or read a book, or pray as you prepare for the meeting. Any one of those options is far better than your blood pressure rising as you duck and weave through traffic in an attempt to be only five minutes and not 15 minutes late.

A place for everything

So far, we've talked about places to put ideas and thoughts. But ideas are not the only thing that you might be trying to remember. You need to know where your physical things are: your car keys, your umbrella, your children's socks, etc. There are many items that your brain might be trying to keep track of in a day.

I try to follow the maxim 'a place for everything, and everything in its place'. My keys are in a pocket in my handbag. I drop my handbag in the same place next to the couch whenever I walk into the house. I have a special drawer in the hall table for library books. I have an electronics drawer in my desk where all cords, chargers and usb keys go. And so on.

Organising and decluttering your house so that you keep track of your belongings and don't waste time looking for them is a other subject that has filled many books, TV shows and podcasts. The two authors that I have found most helpful on the subject are Dana K White and Sandra Felton. I have found their methods to be helpful as I declutter and organise my own house, and I know that an organised house gives me a much clearer brain as I am no longer trying to keep track of every item that I own.

Papers

Paper management can be a big issue in a home. I am sure there are large sections of other books, or even whole books written on the subject. I'm not going to do that, but I'll give you a few tips that have helped me over time.

Firstly, when I empty the mailbox, I go straight to the rubbish bin. All the junk mail gets delivered into the bin straight away. Then, I have a small inbox on my desk and I keep things there that I will have to deal with in the not-too-distant future – things like electricity bills or letters that I will reply to. I have a small filing cabinet next to my desk where I keep medical records, bills and other things that I feel are important to keep. But it is only small, so I can't just keep stacking things in there forever. I keep all the manuals to our electronic goods there, but I try to remember to sort through them regularly so I'm not keeping records on something we threw out ten years ago. Most manuals are now available online so I'm not sure I'll be keeping this folder for much longer. And finally, I keep a shredder near my desk so that I can deal with papers that hold personal information. For many things, like receipts or artwork from my children (when they were small, of course), I take a photograph so that I have a digital record, but I don't need to store the paper itself. I keep as much as I can electronically. Of course, I make sure I back the electronic record up in a couple of places so that it doesn't get lost.

The trick with paper is to keep the piles small. In fact, the trick I keep reading about is to keep the piles nonexistent – to have an action file instead of a pile. That sounds really good, but I haven't made it work for me yet. What does work for me is opening mail next to a bin, and putting any tasks that turn up in the mail onto my calendar so that I am electronically reminded to pay the bill or RSVP to the invitation that is sitting in my inbox.

When you limit the number of places that you keep your thoughts, reminders or papers, you limit the number of places that you have to look. If I remember writing down a thought, I know that it will be in the little book at my bedside, the little book in my handbag, or in my Evernote app on my phone. I don't need to look through many scraps of paper or search every drawer on my desk. I have limited the number of brain buckets that I put things in and this has helped me to keep focused on my unique mission and better able to serve others.

Activities

What are three 'next actions' that you can take to increase the organisation in your house? How can you decrease the number of 'brain buckets' that you have? Is there some decluttering you could do to decrease the number of things you need to remember?

1.

2.

3.

CHAPTER FOURTEEN
Rewards

"*Work is not man's punishment. It is his reward and his strength and his pleasure.*"
– George Sand

"*Chocolate is the first luxury. It has so many things wrapped up in it: deliciousness in the moment, childhood memories, and that grin-inducing feeling of getting a reward for being good.*"
– Mariska Hargitay

How do you motivate yourself?

I have a special talent: I can know what I want to do, I can believe God wants me to do it, I can seriously desire to do it, and I can still not get it done.

For example, I have known since 2014 that I want to be a writer. I want to write and sell books for a living. Writing, both books like this one, and also fiction (which you can find at rjamos.com) is something that I strongly desire to do, and something that I believe God wants me to do.

However, do I wake up in the morning and joyfully sit at my computer and pound out thousands of words each day? No.

That was a surprise, to be honest. I thought that I would just write. That it wouldn't take any special effort or willpower on my part, that if I was given the time to do it I would just do it. But I haven't found that to be the case. There are many different ways to distract myself and all of them give me a dopamine boost and the instant gratification that writing just doesn't give.

Scrolling social media is fun, it's easy, it requires no effort on my part, and it also tricks my brain into thinking I'm accomplishing something when I seriously am not.

Writing is something I love, and something I feel called to do. But the actual writing requires thought and energy, and then there's the imposter syndrome to work through (he/she/the AI chatbot could probably write this better than me. What do I have to say anyway?). There's no guarantee that after hours of work I will produce anything worthwhile, and there's no guarantee that I'll sell any books either.

Writing either gives delayed gratification or very little gratification, and I need to cope with that if there is ever a chance of me being a good writer.

You might feel similarly. You might know that there is something that you love to do, you might know it's something God wants you to do, and yet, it's difficult to actually get down and do the thing, and you find yourself putting it off.

How do we motivate ourselves?

One thing I've noticed with children is that the closer a punishment is to the natural consequences of their actions, the better they respond to that discipline. For example, when our daughter was throwing a tantrum (at age three or four) we would tell her that she wasn't being very good company and that she should go to her room until she could behave better. She is an extrovert. She absolutely loves company. So she would walk up the hallway, touch the bedroom door, and walk back down with a smile pasted onto her tear-stained face. 'I happy now,' she would say. And she would be.

If a child spills a glass of juice, it is much more suitable to help the child get a cloth and mop up the spill than it is to confiscate their favourite toy. The discipline needs to relate to the behaviour.

If a teenager refuses to put their dirty clothes in the dirty washing basket, then the suitable consequence is that the teenager has no clean clothes to wear to school. This may bother the teenager, but also, they may be perfectly happy to wear dirty clothes for a second or third time. In that case, the parent could stay with the teenager while they pick up their own clothes, take them to the laundry and put a load of washing on for themselves. The discipline is a consequence of the actions.

Rewards also are more meaningful when they are a consequence of the actions of the child. When a child helps with baking, an extra cookie is a beautiful reward. When a child puts their toys away, they can have extra reading time with Dad before bed.

This type of parenting is hard work and time-consuming, but it often has excellent results.

In the same way, adults respond to the consequences of our actions. If we strip the bed and choose to delay remaking the bed, then the consequences are that we either have to make the bed at bedtime when we're tired and grumpy, or we have to sleep on an unmade bed. It's a consequence that might make us more eager to promptly make the bed the next time.

Rewards are the same. The reward for the work of making the bed is sleeping in a comfortable freshly made bed. The reward for cooking a meal is eating a delicious dinner. The reward for cleaning the bathroom is a sparkling clean bathroom.

When I started writing, people would tell me to make sure I rewarded myself for finishing the book. But there was a problem with that. The question is, when is a book really finished? Are we talking about the first draft – a draft that often is filled with plot holes and 'fill in name here' placeholders? Or the final draft? Or when a polished draft goes to the editor? Or when I've done the editor's corrections but now it needs to go to the proofreader? Do I reward myself when the first copy is printed? Or when I have many copies printed but I'm now working on the marketing aspect? Like many life projects, there isn't really a satisfactory ending point where I feel like giving myself a reward.

And what sort of reward should I give? As I watch my health and sugar intake, rewarding myself with cake or ice-cream is not helpful for long-term goals. And when the budget is tight, booking a cruise or buying a new trinket might be an impossibility.

I'm beginning to think that if you can rejoice in actually doing the work, that's best. Knowing that you've done what God wanted you to do, that's a reward that you can really relish. There's the satisfaction of ticking off a to-do list. There's the joy of being ready for the thing that's coming up. There's the joy of living with the consequences of a job done well. There's the joy of speaking into someone's life, or being there as an encouragement when they need you.

For Christians, we work for the Lord and hope that at the end of our lives we hear him saying, 'Well done good and faithful servant. Enter into the joy of your Master.'

Yeah, yeah. All that delayed gratification isn't getting me off the couch.

Yes, sometimes we need a bit of a kickstart.

One way that I have helped myself get started on particularly hard tasks is with a reward chart. Yes, a chart that I put a sticker on every time I do the thing. If I write 500 words, I give myself a sticker. Once I get my 20 stickers or whatever, I get the reward. What reward? My rewards have varied from a chocolate bar to three days away on a writing retreat and everything in between.

Reward charts are a good tool to get you started on your journey, but they are not, in my experience, a long-term tool. Even when used to motivate children, they seem to work for about two weeks and then stop working and you need to try something else.

I think the charts stop working because the reward at the end of the chart is removed from the work you are doing to receive the reward. What does eating chocolate have to do with writing? Not a whole lot. I mean, I haven't tried, but I reckon you could produce a whole book without even touching any chocolate. I'm sure it's possible.

Another problem with reward charts for adults is that … we're adults. We might decide that we can have ice cream after we clean the house, and then, we might change our minds and have the ice cream first. I mean, who is going to know? Who is going to care?

So use reward charts and unrelated rewards to motivate yourself if you really need a kickstart. But just be aware that it's not going to work long-term. You'll need to find more intrinsic motivation as you go, and you probably will find it as you take the time to do the thing that gives you life. Once you get over the major hurdle and get started, the work itself will reward you.

Accountability buddies

If you're having trouble motivating yourself by yourself, then maybe you need to have someone else to be accountable to. Someone you can report back to. Someone who will kindly and gently hold a mirror up to you so that you can see whether you're meeting your goals or not. Choose this person carefully. They need to be truthful with you, but also kind.

My personality type means that I respond more strongly when someone else asks me to do something than when I require it of myself. That can mean that I put my own goals (writing books) behind anything that anyone else asks me to do. And that's not healthy. I have found that I need to be responsible to someone who cares about whether or not I'm meeting my own goals. I am blessed that Moz is happy to take that role. I tell him what I want my writing goals to be, and then I have him hold me to them. If I don't write, I am not only letting myself down, but I am also letting him down and that helps me to make time to do this thing that I love and that I feel I am called to do.

This is not about feeling guilt or shame. It is possible that if I were not accountable to someone else, I would not notice that I wasn't reaching my goals. I might just excuse myself week after week for not doing the thing I feel God is asking me to do. I would find excuses that I would call 'reasons' and probably I would also find quite sensible reasons to avoid doing my writing. However, having someone else to be accountable to means that I notice my own behaviour.

The behaviour, the things you actually do, shows you what you truly believe to be important. If week after week I didn't do any writing, my behaviour would be telling me that the writing wasn't actually of great importance to me. I would expect Moz, as an accountability buddy, to reflect that to me. Then I would need to decide whether or not I really wanted to write. Perhaps my behaviour would show me that something else was more important. Sometimes these big ideas are easier to see when you have to explain your behaviour to someone else.

An accountability buddy might also help you to see that the goals you are setting for yourself are unrealistic. That you are aiming too high, or trying to achieve too much in the time that you have in this season. They might help you to reassess and set new goals that are realistic and achievable in the time you have.

What goals should you set?

This is a trial and error process. I know that's annoying, I want to have a fail-safe plan from day one too. But we need to be a little patient with ourselves and find out what works. You need to find out what works for you, individually, with your life circumstances, your energy levels and your motivation.

Say I decide that I want to write a book, and that I'm going to write 4,000 words each day. But as I work towards it, clearing my calendar and scheduling writing time, saying no to other things and motivating myself with a sticker chart and doing everything I know how, I still only manage to write 500 words a day. That would be a little discouraging. I would be tempted to give up writing altogether.

But I wouldn't need to give up. I would only need to adjust my daily goal.

There's a famous Leo Burnett quote, 'When you reach for the stars you may not quite get one, but you won't come up with a handful of mud either'.

But I think that beating yourself up because you're not reaching an unrealistic goal can be almost as bad as the mud.

We don't need to have a perfect plan on day one. We can constantly reassess and tweak and change our goals. What works on one week, might be too much or too little the next week. You might need to take other things out of your schedule or simplify your life so that you can meet your goal, or you might need to change your goals. It really depends on your own life situation.

A goal should stretch you, it should make you work for it. But if you find that you consistently don't hit your goals week after week then that's more than a stretch, and there is a risk that the constant disappointment may break you. If you find that you are consistently not meeting your goal, reduce your expectations, make a smaller goal and try again.

Do I deserve a reward?

I could be wrong, but I think we are more inclined to be too hard on ourselves than to be too easy. We are more inclined to label ourselves 'lazy' than 'exhausted'. We tend to think that if we just try harder and beat ourselves up more, then we will get more done. And that's just not true.

Instead, let's take the time to rejoice in a job well done. To give ourselves a metaphorical pat on the back when we've done a hard thing. To smile in satisfaction when we cross something off our list.

Let's not always look at the mountain ahead of us, but let's take the time to look at and appreciate the view from the hill we've climbed so far. Let's enjoy the intrinsic reward that we get from doing the work we are meant to do.

And occasionally, let's also treat ourselves to a piece of cake and a celebration with our accountability buddy.

Activities

Write the names of three possible accountability buddies. Then, ask these people whether they will help you in this area. You'll need to explain exactly what you mean, so make a time to meet them for coffee and a chat. We're hoping that one of them will say yes.

1.

2.

3.

Write three goals that you will try to achieve in the next four weeks. Tick them off each week as you achieve them. Were they too easy? Too hard? Or just right?

1.

2.

3.

CHAPTER FIFTEEN
Review

"Success is not final, failure is not fatal: it is the courage to continue that counts."
– Winston Churchill

"You are never too old to set another goal or to dream a new dream."
– C.S. Lewis

Art and technique

Bill Bernbach is regarded as the father of modern advertising. When he was creative director of Grey Advertising in the early 20th century, he wrote to agency management about the frustrations he had with all the ads he was seeing. He said that the technicians in advertising knew all the rules and were great scientists,

> "... but look beneath the technique and what did you find? A sameness, a mental weariness, a mediocrity of ideas. But they could defend every ad on the basis that it obeyed the rules of advertising. It was like worshiping a ritual instead of the God."[42]

Technique is important. Bill Bernbach knew that. And technique is what I've tried to provide in this book. Insights and new ways of thinking, plans and practicalities. But more importantly, life is to be lived. And living is an art.

Let's not live our lives in dry technique, worshipping the rituals. Let's worship our God, a living creative being who can cope with the ups and downs of life and help us through them.

I hope that you can take the ideas in this book and apply them to your unique life. Try them and see how they work, or don't work. Add your own creativity to the ideas and tweak them to work for you. Please let me know what happens when you do – I'm always into learning more and you may change my life for the better with your creative living approach.

Assess and reassess

I love this idea that my goals aren't set in concrete. That I can change them as I need to, as my life or health or family

---

[42]https://www.ideatovalue.com/crea/nickskillicorn/2016/04/legendary-1947-letter-lack-creativity-advertising-even-true-2016/

situation changes. It's ok. This is not failure, it is just living life creatively.

It is always a good idea to check in though, to see how your goals are going. I like to check in on a weekly basis, and then each quarter, and each year. Usually, when I check on my written goals, I can tick some off as done, I can see that I am on the way to achieving others, some goals I will adjust, and the rest I might remove altogether. It's clarifying and helps me to live with more intention.

Review

As well as focusing on the goals and plans, you can stretch your life review a bit wider and check in on more broad life areas.

You can divide your review up into:

- Relationships

Are there specific relationships that are life-giving right now? Are there relationships that are draining? Is there something you can do to change or help with those relationships? (For example, visiting a particularly draining person with a friend.)

- Serving opportunities/work

What serving positions is it time to let go of? What positions would you like to take up? Is it time to take up a position on a committee or a board? Is it time to stop helping out on a particular roster or being part of a particular group?

- Significant projects

How many projects are too many? Are there projects you've been hanging onto that really need to be dropped in the coming year? Is there something you've been thinking about that you'd like to take up?

- Self-care, health and wellness

Do you have your holidays booked for the next year? Are you putting time aside for intentional time with God, with family, and with yourself? Are you taking an intentional sabbath once a week? And don't forget your physical health. Are you getting your 30 minutes of exercise? Are you eating healthy food most of the time?

- Money

Do you need to refresh your budget? Have things changed in this area? Are you putting aside that 10% to give to God first?

- A new thing

Is there something new you want to take up? Is this year the year to branch out to a new idea or hobby or ministry?

Many of the activities that you've already completed from this book will add to your life review. They will help you to see where you are now, where you want to go, and the next steps you need to take to get there.

Your whole life

It can also be valuable to check in on your life as a whole. To look at where you've come from and use that to direct where you're going.

One fantastic idea, from author Daniel Sih,[43] uses Post-It notes (or as I call them, sticky notes) to help with a whole-of-life review. The first part of this technique involves brainstorming: writing down the significant people, places and events in your life. You write one idea on each sticky note. Include things that have happened to you, and things you have done. Write out the good and bad events in your life (you might want to put the bad things on a sticky note of another colour to make

---

[43]Daniel Sih, *Spacemaker: How to Unplug, Unwind & Think Clearly in the Digital Age.*

them stand out). Write about the life events or people that have shaped you. Include anything that you see as significant.

You arrange these sticky notes in a logical sequence – a chronological sequence, or maybe in life stages, or any order or set of segments that seems right to you.

When you look at this sequence, you can start to see patterns. You can see how your life has been tracking. You can see how God has been transforming you, and how he has used different situations in your life to bring you to who you are now.

From there, you can dream about the future more effectively. Sih recommends that you write your dreams and ideas for the future on more sticky notes. Once again, just brainstorm. There are no wrong answers here. However, this will show you the direction you're going or want to go and help you to set goals for your future.

Your life story

Another method for reviewing your life is to write a story – your story. You don't have to worry about getting the chronology correct in this story, or even having all the details in there. But you can write about the significant times in your life. You can think of yourself as the main character and write how the events of your life have helped you to change direction or to grow. You can write about how you made key decisions or gained key insights.

You may be more of an artist than a writer, and may want to draw a comic of your life, or a set of pictures that show the major ideas and events. That's great. Or you might want to crack out the play dough and make sculptures. The idea is to make this review creative, tapping in to the emotions and deeper themes that run through your story, helping you to see what God has been doing and where you're headed.

Writing out your story may help you see where you've come from and where you are going.

Future plans

I like to take January to do this sort of life assessment and to make plans for the year ahead. It's a good use of a month that tends to be quiet work-wise for me. It's great to jump into the year ahead with some idea of what I'm intending to achieve in that year. But as we look into the future, it can be helpful to look beyond just the next year. I guess this is why all interviewers ask you to tell them where you see yourself in the next five years.

Dave Evans, the EA of Design Thinking at Stanford says that you should have not one, but three five-year plans.[44]

The first is a plan for where you'll be in five years if you keep following the path you're on now.

The second is a plan for if you take a sharp right turn – work that's related to what you're doing now, but in a different direction.

And the third plan is where you dream about something wild. Something you would do if time and money were no object and you knew you wouldn't fail. What would your five-year plan be then?

Having these three plans in your mind will help you to make decisions as opportunities present themselves. They'll help you to see opportunities that you didn't know were there before.

[44]Quoted by Michael Lindsay in his book *Hinge Moments.*

Activities

Review the different areas of your life:

- Relationships
- Serving opportunities/work
- Significant projects
- Self care, health and wellness
- Money
- A new thing

What are your three five-year plans?

1. If things go according to plan, in five years I will …

2. If things take a sharp turn, in five years I will …

3. If time and money were no object and there was no way I could fail, in five years I would …

Farewell

It is time to put down this book and to walk into your future, to take steps along the path in front of you, to start doing the good works that God planned in advance for you to do. As you do, I hope that at least some of what I've passed on in this book will be helpful to you. I hope that you're living in shalom, that you're running the race set out for you, that you are feeling God's blessing on your life. I hope that you're starting to say no to things that don't fit you and that you're rejoicing more in saying yes to the things that are really yours to do, that fit your unique gifts, skills and personality.

But I hope most of all that you know that whatever you do, you are valuable as you are. You are precious. God loves you with an amazing unconditional love, just the way you are, right now.

> May you work joyfully in the season you are in, may you live peacefully through the different rhythms of life, may you step boldly into success that suits you, and may you grow ever closer to God who created you to be the unique and delightful being that you are.

Join my newsletter at ruthamos.com.au to stay connected, to receive links to my blog and podcast, and to find out about my online course. You can support me at patreon.com/QuietLife for as little as $1 a month.

Please email me at ruth@ruthamos.com.au if you would like me to come and speak at your church or organisation.

Milton Keynes UK
Ingram Content Group UK Ltd.
UKHW042222180324
439698UK00005B/396

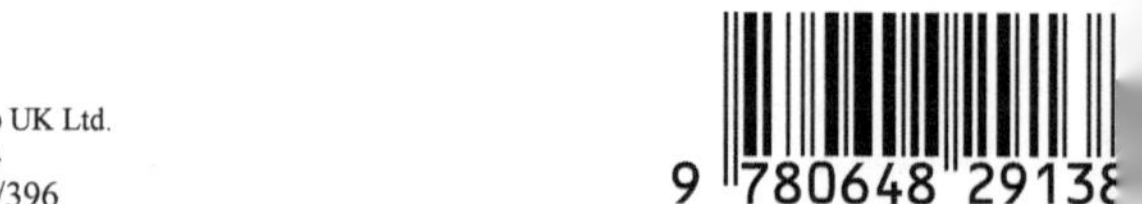